Beginner's Guide to
Collecting Antique Furniture

# Beginner's Guide to Collecting Antique Furniture

PATRICK MACNAGHTEN

HIPPOCRENE
BOOKS, INC.

HIPPOCRENE BOOKS

North Cheek.

All Rights Reserved. For information write:
Hippocrene Books, Inc.
171 Madison Avenue, New York, N.Y. 10016

First published in Great Britain 1973 by
Pelham Books Ltd
52 Bedford Square, London WC1

First published in the United States in 1973
Library of Congress Catalog Number
ISBN 0 88254 049 1

Printed in Great Britain

TO

Christabel Lady Aberconway
from whom I have learned so much

# Contents

# Illustrations

Most of the pieces of furniture shown in the illustrations are superb examples of the respective periods at their finest.

At first a collector will be fortunate if he can find – or afford – such wonderful pieces. But I have chosen them because they are the standard to aim at – the criterion against which more easily obtainable pieces should be judged. Happily, plainer pieces, particularly those of the 18th century, nearly always bear something of the genius which inspired the best – the courtiers copied the king.

I am indebted to those who supplied these illustrations and who took such pains to provide pictures which so accurately reflect the text. These generous people are—

Hotspur Limited.

H. W. Keil Limited.

Phillips of Hitchin (Antiques) Limited.

Spink and Son Ltd.

Denys Wrey Limited.

I cannot name the private owners who have provided illustrations as they wish to remain anonymous, but I am no less grateful to them for sharing their treasures.

*Between pages 140 and 144*

# CHAPTER ONE

# How Collecting Began

A HUNDRED years ago when people spoke of an 'antique' they meant what we call an antiquity – a statue, a piece of pottery or glass dating back to the early civilisations of Greece, Rome or Egypt. An antique was something thousands of years old, certainly not a piece of furniture from a few generations back.

It was not until the end of the 19th century that interest in what we call antique furniture began to awaken. Previously it had been the newest furniture which was most sought after and what we value as antique was simply regarded as old-fashioned. The attitude towards furniture was much the same as it was – and still is – towards clothes. To keep up with the changes in fashion, those who could afford to, replaced their existing furniture with the latest models long before it was worn out. Fortunately for us the old furniture still had a value, albeit a small one, and the owners did not burn it or break it up. Instead they sold it to people who could not afford new, gave it away to a poor relation, or relegated it to the attics, cellars or barns of their spacious houses and estates. Our ancestors must have been great hoarders, and with the space they had available, why not?

The result of all this was that good antique furniture became spread throughout Britain. Farmhouses and cottages in the country, and modest villas and terrace houses in the towns all had their share of the old-fashioned, little-regarded stuff. When people began to take an interest in antique furniture many a cottager was amazed to find that the funny old table which grandfather had bought for sixpence at the sale at the big house had suddenly become worth several pounds.

The reason for the sudden interest in antiques is a simple one. Throughout the second half of the 19th century the production of furniture became more and more mechanised. While it had not yet reached the scale of mass-production, the individual craftsman was facing increasing competition from the factories. Consequently he could no longer spend the time needed to make a really fine piece of furniture without pricing himself out of the market. The skill was still there but the time certainly was not.

Simultaneously designers had begun to turn up the pattern books of a century before, and to produce furniture along the lines laid down then. This was only one of the fashions of the late 19th century, but it was important enough to accustom people to the look of furniture as it had been a hundred years before. From this it was a natural progression to think about not only the designs but the actual furniture of a previous age. It had become difficult to find good new furniture and people started to look elsewhere for quality. The obvious place to look was in the attic where the old stuff had been gathering dust for years. When they took it down and cleaned it the beauty which had been ignored for so long became apparent. Gradually antique furniture began to be appreciated, not just as a substitute for new, but as something desirable in its own right.

It was not that the late Victorians and Edwardians were more perceptive or more enlightened than their fathers and grandfathers. It was simply that the supply of newly-made furniture of the finest quality had dried up. If it had not they – and we today – would have gone on buying the newest furniture, just as our ancestors did. In the 17th century people considered Elizabethan furniture to be hopelessly out-of-date, and the Georgians thought, not without reason, that the furniture of their own day was infinitely superior to anything which had been made before.

If conditions today were the same as they were in the 18th century we would probably still be making wonderful furniture. But conditions are not the same, and as far as one can be certain of anything in the future, they never will be. Mid-20th century furniture is well designed – some better designed than others – but the vast majority of it is mass-produced and consequently it has to be simple. You cannot hold up a production line for a fortnight while somebody carves the leg of a chair. Furthermore, labour is more expensive than materials. In the great days of cabinet-making it was the other way round. It made sense, when you had a piece of wood which had cost a comparatively large sum, to pay a man a comparatively small sum to spend long hours working on it. It is not within the scope of this book to discuss social implications. All we need do is be thankful that the result was something which we ourselves can enjoy while being sorry for any sweated labour that there may have been.

This is not to say that all present-day furniture is inferior to antiques. There is good modern furniture and there are bad antiques. Also many things which make life easier now were unknown to our ancestors. The low armchairs produced today are a great deal more comfortable than anything they had. The long, low coffee-tables which we find so convenient were unknown in previous centuries (except perhaps to the Ancient Greeks and Romans whose long, low tables were bigger than ours, and not used for coffee. Their orgies were bigger, too.). Kitchen units with plastic tops cause less trouble than pine tables which had to be scrubbed. Interior-sprung mattresses are more conducive to a good night's rest than anything the 18th – or any other – century produced. An electric fire does its job better than a charcoal brazier. A television set gives better – or anyway more varied – entertainment than a magic lantern, and I am very glad that I am not writing this book with a quill pen by the light of a candle.

One can overdo the worship of antiques if one tries to substitute them for more convenient furniture. However, much antique furniture serves the purpose for which it was made just as efficiently for you and me as it did for its original owner. In other words, it is functional, and it has the enormous advantage of being beautiful. It is rare for the sensible and the enjoyable to unite harmoniously, but they do when we collect antique furniture.

Furniture has big advantages for the collector. It is not as easily broken as glass or porcelain, nor as easily stolen as silver and pictures. It is more attractive to the eye than postage stamps which somebody else has licked, and provided it is treated with ordinary care, it does not deteriorate with use. It is much nicer to live with than stocks and shares, and although it does not pay dividends often it beats them when it comes to capital gains.

Almost all antiques increase in value, though there are fluctuations when a certain period is out of fashion. But if we look back over the seventy or eighty years during which people have been actively collecting antiques we can see that a fall is followed, sooner or later, by a rise. Oak furniture was in fashion in the 1920s but twenty years later you could hardly give it away. It came into fashion again in the 1960s and prices soared. In the 1930s everybody regarded Regency furniture with a very cold eye (unless somebody persuaded them that it was 'Sheraton') but by the 1950s they were queuing up to buy it.

I have a pair of footstools made about 1870. Twenty years ago people, seeing them for the first time, would either politely avert their eyes, or draw in their breath with a sharp hiss of horror. Now they croon and drool over them.

Funiture, then, is subject to changes in fashion, like most other things. A certain period becomes popular, and then the public appetite becomes sated. But one cannot trace a pattern, except insofar as periods which have been out of fashion for a long time are probably due to come in again. But this is not entirely reliable. The next stage may be forwards just as easily as backwards. A period which has hitherto been completely ignored may suddenly come galloping up, though as most of them have had their day, it is more likely to be some esoteric style which does not conveniently fit into any recognised period.

If, by luck or inspired guesswork, you can foresee what is going to be in fashion ten years ahead you stand to make a lot of money. On the other hand, if you buy at the top of the market when a certain style has already had a long run, it may be more than ten years before the wheel comes round again and you can make a profit. But in the meantime you have something you like to look at. *What* you like looking at is entirely a matter of personal taste, and there is no absolute in taste any more than there is in art. One can, I suppose, train oneself to like what other people tell one to like, and there is no doubt that one can learn to appreciate the finer details which originally escaped one. But taste is as ephemeral as fashion. Or rather, unless you have formed your own taste you will be swayed by fashion, which comes to the same thing. What I think one discovers is that one's taste may develop with increased knowledge, but that is only a widening of horizons. The things which appeal naturally to one at twenty will still appeal at sixty. Possibly to a lesser degree, possibly to a greater, but they will still appeal.

I suggest that it is more important to know what you don't like than what you do. If you can judge what is, to your own eye or mind intrinsically bad, the good will stand in sharper relief. Beauty may be in the eye of the beholder, but ugliness just as much. So I try to base my dislikes on rational grounds. For instance, I dislike those Victorian chairs whose legs have corkscrew twists going in opposite directions because they appear to me to be trying to screw themselves into the floor. But this is mere prejudice. I am on much surer ground if I dislike them because the spiky coat-of-arms (probably bogus) sticks into my back and hurts.

Logically I should dislike those tables of the late 18th century whose legs are slenderly tapered that they can scarcely stand up. But in fact, against all reason, I simply love them.

Taste is a highly personal, individual matter. As long as something makes you happy don't, I beg you, mind what anybody else thinks.

# CHAPTER TWO

# A Brief Survey

FURNITURE no doubt began when the first caveman rolled
a log of wood into his cave and sat on it. Probably the next
step was to support a flat stone on a couple of nearly round
ones to form the ancestor of a table. The history of furniture
is the history of civilisation, with all its fascinating tale of
development from barbarity to sophistication, with the occasional lapse into decadence on the way.

One of the less disagreeable characteristics of *homo sapiens*
is his innate instinct to create a home and to surround himself
with objects which please him. Some are better at it than others,
but we all try. Take, for example, King Ahasuerus who, the
*Book of Esther* tells us 'reigned from India even unto Ethiopia,
over an hundred and seven and twenty provinces'. His home
may not have been a very happy one but it was unquestionably
very grand. 'White, green, and blue hangings, fastened with
cords of fine linen and purple to silver rings and pillars of
marble : the beds were of gold and silver, upon a pavement of
red, and blue, and white, and black, marble.'

How one would love to know what the gold and silver beds
looked like! But the written description is enough to tell us that
the art of furniture making was well advanced in Biblical times.
For many of the ancient civilisations there are carvings and
designs on pottery to show us what the furniture was like. I
have always thought it odd that pottery has survived whereas
furniture, which one would expect to be more durable, has not.

The earliest furniture of which we can form a clear idea is
the Ancient Egyptian. This is because they never really accepted

the doctrine that 'you can't take it with you' and they filled their tombs with objects which had been useful in this life, in the lively hope that if they would not actually be useful in the next life at least they would provide the dead with familiar surroundings. The Ancient Egyptians also tried to make these arrangements permanent by putting a curse on anybody who should desecrate the tombs.

Despite the curses, enough tombs have been opened to provide a detailed picture of life in Ancient Egypt where, more than three thousand years ago, the art of furniture-making had reached a high standard, both constructionally and aesthetically. X-shaped folding stools had leather seats, four-legged stools rush seats, and the legs of the more elaborate pieces were carved to represent the hooves and paws of animals. Some furniture was inlaid with gold, mother-of-pearl, ivory, pottery, or semi-precious stones and metals.

The elegant flowing lines of the chairs depicted on Ancient Greek tombs are strongly reminiscent of the Egyptian. Indeed, it would be remarkable if this were not so as the civilisations overlapped. Throughout history this pattern of development is repeated time and again, a rising culture adopts and adapts the best ideas of the waning one. Thus the Greeks drew on the experience of the Egyptians, the Romans on that of the Greeks, and gradually the tide of taste, knowledge and art spread slowly westward over Europe.

Other ancient cultures, such as those of the Far East and Central and South America were too remote to have any effect on the European peoples who had never heard of them.

When Julius Caesar invaded Britain in 55 B.C. he found a primitive race who had not progressed much since their ancestors swung by their tails from trees. The disparity between the highly cultured Romans lolling about on inlaid couches and the savage natives darting round daubed with woad was too great. The Britons simply could not swallow the medicine of civilisation however much good they were told it would do them. They were not ready for it. When the Romans sailed away their culture went with them. Their gracious houses crumbled into ruin, grass grew over the paving stones of their roads, and the Britons sighed with relief and relapsed into squalor.

The Normans, though probably considerably less couth than the Romans, were equally shocked at the primitive state of what by this time had become the Anglo-Saxons. But this time there was a difference. The Normans did not go away, as the Romans had done. They steadily absorbed, and were absorbed by, the native race, and the tentative beginnings of English culture started to emerge. The Normans built splendid cathedrals and fine castles, the one for worshipping in, the other as fortresses – neither for living in. It is true that they inhabited their castles but the primary function was military not domestic and those readers who remember the Second World War will know that armed men are hard on furniture.

It was not really until about the year 1500 that houses ceased to be fortresses and England became comparatively peaceful. Heads could still fall at the drop of an axe but provided you avoided crime and politics – especially politics – you could reasonably expect to die in your bed. And if you were lucky enough to be rich it would be a magnificent bed at that. But how long you might expect to live was quite another matter. Sanitary conditions were appalling, not to say nauseating, and medical science was in its infancy. To reach old age you needed to be tough, and more, to be the fittest was no guarantee of survival – you had to be lucky as well.

But in spite of the health hazards, England under the Tudors was prosperous and relatively peaceful. Consequently people were able to spend lavishly on their homes and the crude furniture of the Middle Ages gave place to much more elaborate and ingenious styles. The Court was the fount of all power and most wealth so naturally it had an enormous influence on the furniture of the time. Most of the early Tudor furniture looks as if it had come out of a church, to this day the four-legged stools of the period are usually known as 'coffin stools', food cupboards had pointed Gothic arches for ventilation, like miniature church windows, and chests made for the home were exactly the same as those made to hold ecclesiastical vestments.

The reason for this was that the greater part of the country's learning and skill was to be found in the abbeys and monasteries. If you wanted to build a house you would apply to the abbot for a brother who understood these mysteries to come and act as foreman to your own unskilled workers and the same monk or friar – or one like him – would make or supervise the making of your furniture.

The Roman Catholic Church played a very important part in the secular as well as the religious life of the country and Henry VIII's Dissolution of the Monasteries disrupted far more than its religious significance might suggest. Italy was enjoying that wonderful resurgence of artistic creation known as the Renaissance, and Henry's split with Rome cut off the influence of the Renaissance as with a tap. The constant to-ing and fro-ing between England and Rome which had been such a feature of the Middle Ages, ceased abruptly. It was at least a hundred years before England caught up with the architectural styles of the Renaissance and in the meantime the English had to make do with the watered-down and mis-interpreted styles which filtered through from France and the Netherlands.

The result was that the furniture, like the architecture, of Late Tudor times developed a peculiarly English style. Furniture always reflects the spirit of its age, and the Elizabethan was an ebullient one. Ostentation was considered a virtue and wealth was something to be proud of, and displayed. Furniture was decorated with vigorous carving, sometimes gilding, often inlay.

But rich though the furniture was it was scarce. When the Court moved from one palace to another the furniture – or much of it – went too, and anybody who has ever moved house knows that a removal takes a heavy toll of breakable objects. The wonder is not that so little Tudor furniture has survived – rather it is marvellous that any has survived at all. For all the nonsense of its ornamentation, it was very solidly made. The great majority of Tudor furniture which still exists is made of oak. Oak is an extremely durable wood and it has lasted the course better than most others. But it would be a mistake to think that it was the only wood used at the time. In the same way that local materials dictated what houses should be built of, so furniture makers used the woods which were readily available – oak, beech, elm, and the fruit-woods were all employed. It is just that the furniture made from oak has lasted better.

When it is young oak is a golden colour so Elizabethan houses were light and colourful places, not at all dark and gloomy as would be a house furnished entirely with Tudor oak today.

As the 16th century ended the styles of furniture became more restrained and rather finicky. This is a pattern which is repeated throughout the history of furniture. A style starts vigorous and clear and then degenerates into confused and sketchy detail, as if the maker had forgotten what he was trying to do, and had lost heart anyway. They still didn't know much about what was going on in Italy. While Shake-speare was in his teens Andrea Palladio was building at Vicenza what must be the most beautiful theatre in the world and is arguably the most beautiful secular building. Shakespeare's own glorious plays had to be put on in the dreary hovel which was the best London could provide. English literature had scaled the heights while English furniture was only fussing about in the foothills.

There were exceptions, of course. The state beds, the furni-ture completely covered in silver, the chairs with velvet cushions shone like a bright light (or stuck out like a sore thumb, whichever way you like to look at it) in the reign of James I.

The most promising development in the early 17th century was Inigo Jones's visit to Italy. For the first time an English-man fully comprehended what the Renaissance was all about. He came back full of enthusiasm and began to plan a palace for Whitehall which, if it had ever been built, would have rivalled Versailles. But the times were against him. The Renais-sance had only had a minimal influence on English architecture and almost none on English furniture when the Civil War loomed darkly on the horizon. It is one of the ironies of history that that most cultured of monarchs Charles I (he formed one of the finest collections of painting there has ever been) stepped on to the scaffold from a window of the Banqueting House, the only part of Inigo Jones's grandiose plan for Whitehall which was completed.

During the Civil War everybody was far too busy to worry about the finer arts, such as furniture making, and during the ensuing Commonwealth only the very rich and powerful dared to. A regime which banned Maypole dancing and considered Christmas puddings sinful was hardly likely to encourage – or even countenance – lavish display in the homes of its police state. Cromwellian furniture is plain, dull and utilitarian. And made of oak.

The Restoration of Charles II in 1660 was a milestone in the development of English furniture, as it was in English history. Charles and his ramshackle Court had spent their exile in France and the Netherlands and when they got home they brought Continental ideas with them. After a long period of doubt and gloom the sun suddenly began to shine and the nation responded like a blossoming flower. The only snag was that there wasn't much money about. But they all did their best – and what a splendid best it was! The 18th century sacrificed comfort to beauty, the 19th beauty to comfort, but the late 17th century triumphantly combined the two.

Both the French and the Dutch had long been using walnut for furniture – as had the Italians – and Restoration England joyfully accepted it. Walnut, unlike oak, can be cut into very thin sheets whose graceful grain makes ideal veneers, and this property was fully exploited. Not content with that, exciting as it was, the English furniture makers also adopted the Continental fashion for marquetry. But walnut has its drawbacks. Wide solid planks tend to warp and veneers lift and crinkle if you put anything hot on them. Therefore, oak was still used for the types of furniture such as tables and chairs, for which it was most suitable. To appreciate the full beauty of walnut's delicate grain you have to see it close to and consequently it was ideally suited to the small, cosy rooms of the period.

23

Simultaneously in America there was a switch from the forms of furniture which the early settlers had known before they left England and which had been carried on almost unchanged for nearly a century. By the last quarter of the 17th century the settlements on the East Coast were flourishing and prosperous. The fine houses being built then were furnished with money and taste but the styles were imported from Europe. Oddly enough, it was in the country districts, far removed from the fashionable seaboard, that the beginnings of an individual American style appeared – a sturdy and vigorous style created by a sturdy and vigorous people, which was to reach its apotheosis a hundred years later.

In England, where the uncertain climate militates against the regular progress of a tree's growth, the walnut trees did not produce the even grain necessary for fine cabinet work. In any case, walnut trees had not been grown extensively in this country and hastily planted saplings could not reach maturity in time to meet the demand. Consequently the bulk of walnut was imported from southern France. But the outbreak of the War of the Spanish Succession put a stop to that and by the time peace came in 1713 walnut was very scarce owing to the death of many of the trees in the exceptionally hard winter of 1709. In 1720 the French banned the export of the wood altogether. England could still draw on Holland and Spain but the major part of the import was from Virginia. Virginian walnut is darker and with a less lively grain, not as suitable for veneers. Hence much early 18th century furniture was made from walnut in the solid, enlivened with bold carving and shapes of architectural outline.

An even harder wood, mahogany, had long been known in England but the cost of importing it from the West Indies had hitherto made it prohibitive. Now, however, it could compete on equal terms with walnut.

The coming of mahogany coincided with the greatest period of English cabinet-making. The Italian Renaissance had at last reached England and in a period of prosperity huge and magnificent houses sprang up in a style which had been formed in Italy some two hundred years earlier. These great mansions

24

called for a vast amount of furniture and the English cabinet-makers rose splendidly to the occasion. Thomas Chippendale has given his name to this period but in fact he was only one among many, all of them superb craftsmen and some of them great artists. Chippendale's own influence was due to his publication of very successful books of designs, by far the most important of numerous similar works of reference which appeared in the mid-18th century. It was because of these books that the style of the period is so uniform. New ideas promulgated in London were almost immediately adopted throughout the country. This is, of course, not to say that the more conservative furniture-makers did not continue with the familiar styles of their youth. Also, all furniture was commissioned, and there were conservative customers as well. But anybody who wanted to be in the fashion had ample opportunity of discovering what the fashion was.

Chippendale's *The Gentleman and Cabinet Maker's Director* appeared in its first edition in 1754, and the timing could not have been better. The purity of Palladianism was beginning to pall, and people were beginning to look around for something more entertaining. Chippendale abundantly supplied this need. He produced designs in three styles – Rococo (a contraction of the French words for rocks and shells), Chinese, and Gothic. Some of his Rococo designs were too bizarre for anybody to like and too complicated for anybody to make, but in simplified form they were immensely popular. It is really astonishing to see what a good craftsman could do with wood, from carving it to look like ribbon to estimating the precise shape and size of leg to support a given weight.

The styles of 'Chinese Chippendale' bear practically no relation to the furniture made in China in his or any other time, but nobody minded that. China was on the other side of the world and it was fun to let the imagination run riot. The 'Chinese taste' was not as universal as the Rococo but it was amusingly different. So, too, was the Gothic. If the Chinese style stemmed from fantasy the Gothic was pure romanticism – a recreation of medieval mystery. But all these styles gave place to a new classicism. Robert Adam, the great architect of the 1760s, designed his elegant interiors down to the last detail, and neatly parcelled them up by having carpets woven to repeat the patterns of his ceilings.

Adam sought his inspiration from classical sources but he applied the details rather than the forms. The beauty of his designs – both of plasterwork and furniture – owes much to exquisite workmanship. Chippendale worked extensively for him, with advantage to both of them.

The great delicacy of Adam's furniture is achieved by a reversion to inlay, but in a different style from that of 17th century marquetry. Formal classical shapes stood out, visually, they were really inlaid, from light coloured satinwood. Adam created rooms of aesthetic perfection, but they expressed his own personality rather than that of his clients. Magnificent showpieces, definitely not homes. Impossible to imagine anybody clumping in in muddy boots and throwing himself down in one of Adam's exquisite chairs.

The next development was the publication in 1788, two years after the author's death, of George Hepplewhite's *The Cabinetmakers' and Upholsterers' Guide*. If Adam was the founder of neo-classicism, George Hepplewhite was its prophet. The designs cover a wide range of furniture, using both mahogany and satinwood. Inlay was popular but a cheaper form of decoration was introduced at this period, painting of swags and flowers in colour. Little regarded at the time, it is now highly prized, and rightly so for it is very delicate and beautiful. There was a strong affinity with French furniture of the period but whereas in France the style ended with brutal abruptness in the Revolution, in England it merged smoothly into the next phase.

The late 18th century saw a new and different style emerge in America. After the Declaration of Independence the Americans were not unnaturally violently anti-British and the last thing they wanted was to copy English furniture. They turned more to France for inspiration and the result was a completely individual American style, happily combining the best of European designs with their own ideas. The result was as robust as English furniture, less mannered than French, and managed to combine sturdiness with flowing lines. It was not until the genius of Duncan Phyfe that American furniture again resembled the European styles.

In England, the massive publication of the volumes of Thomas Sheraton's *Cabinet Makers' and Upholsterers' Drawing Book* over the three years from 1791 formed a fitting development of Hepplewhite's designs. There was the same delicacy but the designs looked stronger, mainly because the graceful curves had given place to equally graceful straight lines. All very clean and free of carving they relied for their interest on the contrast between light satinwood and dark mahogany, on painted decoration, and on thin and delicate inlay of brass.

The first Empire style of France had a strong influence on early 19th century English furniture. Military motifs were freely used, and one can almost hear the drums beating and the trumpets sounding. The renewed interest in Ancient Grecian architecture led to a cold, chaste classicism which would have made the houses rather dull if they had not been filled with the somewhat showy furniture of the Regency period. Whether light or heavy, Regency furniture was always emphatic and its architectural inspiration was culled from Ancient Greek, Egyptian sources and in fact from practically anywhere in the ancient world. The fashionable wood was rosewood which was often inlaid with brass, and there was a strong liking for gilding.

Towards the end of the Regency period furniture took on an unfortunate grossness, and became ponderous. Some of it was fantastic in its elaboration but the delicacy of the late 18th century had gone for good – or rather for bad.

There was a short Indian summer of light and dainty furniture between about 1830 and 1845, but the varied displays in the Great Exhibition of 1851 showed a depressing lack of beauty.

Now, however, there is a swing towards the collecting of Victorian furniture. There was good and bad furniture made in every age, but we are near enough to the 19th century for more of its bad furniture to have come down to us than from any other time. However, collecting is essentially a selective

27

business, so we can concentrate on finding the good Victorian pieces, and some of them are very good indeed.

Much Victorian furniture is heavy, clumsy and ugly but it had the merit of being solidly made. The plainer pieces are often attractive, and many of the smaller objects have great charm.

More furniture was made in the 19th century than in any other, because there were more people. In 1801 the census of England and Wales disclosed a total population of 8,892,536. Ninety years later the figure had risen to just over twenty-nine million. It follows, therefore, that there was a rapidly accelerating demand for furniture and, as always happens when there is a buyer's market, standards fell. It was this scarcity of fine furniture which caused discriminating people to take a closer look at earlier furniture which had previously been discarded. Thus collecting began, which is where we came in.

# CHAPTER THREE

# From the Middle Ages to the Early Tudor Period

LIFE in the Middle Ages must have been extremely uncomfortable, as well as dangerous. A castle was a place from which you sallied forth to fight and to which, if you were lucky, you returned to eat and sleep. Narrow windows were designed more for keeping out arrows than for letting in light and it was not until fairly late on that they had the idea of covering the opening with horn – and later still with glass – to keep out the wind and the rain.

With the entire fighting force and its attendant administrative tail living hugger-mugger in one enormous hall, what little furniture there was had to be completely utilitarian. The floors were covered with rushes and when they became too deeply impregnated with human urine and canine excretion a fresh covering of rushes was laid on the top. Medieval nostrils were not sensitive. In the centre of the hall would be a fire – but not a fireplace. Logs smouldered away, and the smoke drifted all over the place, finally escaping through the windows or simple louvres in the roof. It was thought that this smoke discouraged the fleas, but the men were tougher than their parasites.

They would gobble their food at tables as crude as their manners. The tables were simply roughly hewn boards supported by, but not attached to, trestles, and at night they were propped against the windows to form primitive shutters. People sat on benches or stools, without any backs to them.

The earliest form of chest was just a tree-trunk hollowed

out to form a receptacle and it is strange that the word 'trunk' has come down through the ages with its meaning adapted but more or less unchanged. If you could be transported back in time and say to a medieval peasant 'fetch my trunk' he would know what you were talking about just as well as a modern porter, though he would probably charge you much less for doing it.

From these early chests evolved a type constructed of six boards fastened together with large iron nails and sometimes bound with iron straps.

All this very early furniture is lumped together under the heading 'Gothic' – a dangerously misleading term for the beginner, because, as will be shown later on, there were two distinct revivals in the 18th and 19th centuries. But these later Gothicisms are generally distinguished from the earlier form by being written 'Gothick' or 'Gothic Revival'. Of course no medieval knight, returning from the Crusades, would say to his wife 'Oh by the way, I bought a lovely Gothic chest today', any more than his 19th century equivalent would say 'I've just bought a Victorian house'. The nomenclature of furniture is always later than the furniture itself – except for that funny old-fashioned stuff of the 1950s which was called 'Contemporary' when it was. I do not know – nor greatly care – when the word 'Gothic' was first applied to medieval furniture. But it was probably early in the 18th century, when the fashion for classicism made anything earlier seem uncouth. Certainly it was then used in a derogatory sense as in 'Goths and Vandals'. The Goths have now become respectable but the poor Vandals still have their name applied to hooligans (a much more expressive word) who smash up telephone boxes.

Anyway, I am rather inclined to dodge the issue and call any furniture made before the Tudor period 'archaic'.

It is generally agreed that very little furniture exists today which was made before about 1500, and the term 'Tudor' is applied to stuff made between then and 1600, though often 'Elizabethan' is used for furniture made in or about the reign of the Virgin Queen. It is, however, extremely difficult to date 16th century furniture with any degree of accuracy. It is hard enough, in all conscience, to tell when houses were built unless there is some supporting evidence like household accounts or perhaps a date carved in stone above the entrance. But no household accounts of that period give sufficient details of furniture for us to be able to identify it, even if it does still exist which is unlikely.

If I were to see a piece of furniture with the date 1500 carved on it I would disbelieve it. (Actually I never have, though I have seen plenty bearing a date of sixteen hundred and something.) I regret to say that early dates are nearly always suspect. When, for the last ten years of the 19th century and the first thirty years of the 20th century, people began collecting antique furniture the preference was for Tudor. The Victorians liked ornate furniture and naturally they preferred ornate antiques. Consequently the antique dealers of the day gratified their wishes and carved all sorts of funny ornament on plain Tudor pieces, and often slapped on a spurious date for bad measure. They also, of course, diligently made fakes, and thought of a number which might deceive somebody. Not you, I hope.

I am sorry to take such a gloomy view, but I do not think any prudent collector would be asinine enough to attribute a precise date to any piece of the period ending the early 16th century.

There is, for instance, an interesting table in the Banqueting Hall of Haddon Hall in Derbyshire (open to the public). This Banqueting Hall was built in 1370 (altered since, but not much, and well documented) and the table, which was made for carving on, may well be of the same date. But, equally, it may be a hundred or so years later. You simply can't tell. It is a rough hunk of wood, like a butcher's block, and it has legs, splayed at an angle and stuck in the underside. A narrow oval ditch has been chiselled into the surface to collect the juices from the meat which then ran off through a hole into, presumably, a jug of wood or horn standing on the floor underneath. An ingenious idea, if crudely executed, but who thought of it and when we shall never know. In those early times there were knives and spoons but no forks and instead of plates they used thick slices of bread. The emerging English language was much larded with Norman French and the 'tranche' – slice – has come down to us in the phrase 'a good trencherman'.

The same house contains a fascinating collection of food hutches which probably date from the reign of Henry VII (1485-1509) or possibly a year on either side. These hutches are often called 'dole cupboards' which were specifically those in churches and monasteries in which was kept the food to be doled out to the poor of the parish. However, the same carpenter – who may have been a monk – no doubt made hutches for secular as well as ecclesiastical use and there is no difference in style. As mentioned in Chapter Two, the inhabitants of the religious houses played an important part in the secular life of the country, and they had the knowledge and skills which fitted them to do so.

These early food hutches all follow the same pattern. The boards which form the sides continue unbroken to meet the floor, there are no separate feet. The door is hung on iron strap hinges fitted to the outside. The fronts of the hutches are ventilated by means of holes, quite elaborately carved in either geometrical patterns or Gothic arches reminiscent of church windows.

The food hutch seems to have been an item of furniture peculiar to this period and does not appear later. However, one does occasionally find cupboards of the late 18th century with their double doors (as opposed to the single door of the food hutch) with pierced fretwork. These cupboards, although usually made in unfashionable wood of 'country' style, are rather more elaborate than one would expect them to be if intended to stand in a kitchen. In even quite modest houses of the 18th century dining rooms were usually a long way from kitchens and so possibly it was more convenient to put food which would be wanted at the next meal in a cupboard in the dining room. But the reason for the disappearance of the food hutch in the intervening centuries can only have been because they were unnecessary – food was kept in larders with cold stone or slate shelves. It is only now, in the 20th century that we have reverted to keeping our food in little hutches. Our refrigerators are vastly more suitable to the purpose than the medieval hutches were, but can hardly be called ornamental.

It was about the end of the 15th century that furniture began to emerge as a craft in its own right, the prerogative of joiners, not carpenters. Carpenters fashioned roof timbers, ceilings, and partitions whereas joiners were responsible for the more delicate work such as floors, staircases, panelling and furniture.

The term 'joinery' comes from the method of securing the framework of panels rather than with nails, as previously. At one end of the hall would be a wooden screen separating the main body of the hall from the outer door and the doorways leading to kitchens and pantries. In earlier times these screens had been made of planks of wood which warped and split, but now came much shorter and thinner lengths of timber, held in a joined frame. This panelling was also used to cover the bare stone walls and in its original state it must have given the rooms a much gayer, cosier look.

Right up to about the middle of the 17th century the most usual ornamentation for panels was the ribbed carving known as 'linenfold'. The same type of linenfold panelling is, of course, found in cathedrals and churches where it makes the most effective pew-ends. It is generally supposed that the folded linen motif represents the napkin of the Eucharist and in view of its ecclesiastical origin this seems a reasonable deduction, especially as this form of decoration was not confined to England but is found on furniture made all over Europe.

Another type of carved ornament for a panel was a human profile set in a roundel. Obviously this, whether intended as a portrait or simply as a face, was more difficult to carve than a linenfold, so it is naturally found only on the more important pieces of furniture. It is interesting in that it shows the first glimmerings of the influence of the Italian Renaissance, though I must admit that the standard of the English carving of wood falls a long way below the Florentine carving of marble.

33

The Tudor period was one of comparative peace, and it was no longer necessary to barricade the doors against invaders. Consequently furniture did not have to be constructed with one eye on defence. The joiners could concentrate on making it suitable for its real purpose without having to take into account its effectiveness as a barricade. They set to with a will, and were assured of enthusiastic customers.

The early Tudors, Henry VII and Henry VIII, typified the age in which they lived. Vigorous and ebullient, they were larger than life, just what their subjects expected monarchs to be. In the palaces and great houses it was a time of rapidly accelerating sophistication. Panelling, tapestries or rich designs painted directly on to the plaster in tempera, ornamented the walls, and furniture quickly developed from its early strictly functional form to one of elaborate, not to say gorgeous, decoration. Anybody who was rich displayed his wealth like a battle honour, modesty about possessions was unthinkable, and how better to display wealth than by having the most magnificent houses furnished with the most eye-taking furniture which money could buy.

The habit of putting food on hunks of bread had given place to wooden platters or trenchers but in the houses of the rich food was served on pewter plates. When burnished with sand to a high polish pewter is very decorative, far too good to be shoved away out of sight when not in use. It was, therefore, a logical progression that elaborate pieces of furniture should be made on which the pewter could be shown off. As the name implies, the earliest cupboards had been simply boards or shelves for parking the wooden or horn cups on. But a simple arrangement like that did not appeal to the rich and splendid nobility and merchants of Tudor times. It might be all right for the peasants, who didn't possess any pewter anyway, but not for the upper classes. Their disregard for economy in money applied equally to the consideration of space. A Tudor cupboard takes up an awful lot of room, and even the largest could not have held many pewter plates. (Or gold or silver ones, come to that.) It consisted of a two-tiered structure, the base solid legs and the upper part a shelf with a small space enclosed by a door in the middle. What in modern terms would be called the cupboard – that is the small enclosed part – was useful for holding whatever minor items they did not wish to display. The plates were ranged, standing on their edges, on either side. This sort of furniture is often referred to as a 'Court Cupboard' though the derivation is obscure. Records show that it was in use in the period but it is more likely to indicate the length (i.e. French for short) than a connection with Royalty.

Chairs of the period are rare, as indeed they were in their own time. Only the grandest establishments had them, and then usually only one, for the head of the household. Everybody else sat on stools or benches.

The chair has had, from earliest times, an almost mystical symbolism. A sort of secular altar. The monarch sits on a throne, the chairman of a company is very much the head man, no one sits in the presence of Royalty unless commanded to do so. The bishop's stall in a cathedral is grander than that of any of the other clergy, and so on. Even today the host and hostess will occupy the chairs with arms at the dining table while their guests sit on more humble, armless chairs, whereas in the other rooms of the house it is the guests who are invited to take the most comfortable seats.

Early Tudor chairs were solid affairs, rectangular in shape. The lower part was panelled, as were the arms. The back, also panelled was straight. (It was not until the late 17th century that some bright individual realised that the human spine is curved.) Sometimes the seat was hinged, like a Victorian night-commode, but there was no pot inside, just a space for storing things. These hefty angular chairs were not quite so uncomfortable as they look because there would be a fairly elementary cushion to sit on, a bag stuffed with feathers or wool. Upholstered furniture was unheard of then, but the importance of the man who enjoyed the enviable comfort of the cushion has not diminished with the passage of time. The Lord Chancellor still sits on the Woolsack.

Towards the middle of the 16th century the stern protocol relaxed sufficiently for the ladies of the house to enjoy a modicum of comfort. Special light chairs were made for them, chairs which could be moved about and drawn up to the fire which by this time was laid on a hearth let into a wall. But even this concession had a sting in the tail. These light framed but unpanelled chairs were known as 'caquetoire' – French, gossip.

Antonis Mor's portrait of Queen Mary I shows her sitting, bolt upright, in what must have been a very unusual chair for the time (mid-16th century). It has an upholstered back and the arms, too, are covered with what is probably velvet, and fringed. But such a chair was very exceptional, far beyond the dreams of a subject, let alone a collector over four hundred years later. But at least it shows that they did know how to upholster chairs then, although surviving examples almost all date from some fifty years later. It is a point worth remembering that the more comfortable a chair is the more likely it is to be worn out long before a less comfortable one of the same date.

For ordinary folk the most they could aspire to was a stool. Not the type with splayed legs let into its underside, which was now superseded by a 'joined stool', that is one with straight legs mortised into a frame with the seat on top.

Tables were still fairly plain in Tudor times, although the top was now permanently fixed to the trestle base. They were long and rather narrow and, at least in the great houses, a second table would be set at right angles to the first, to form a 'T'. The head of the household and his lady would sit side by side at the top table, facing down the stem of the 'T' at which sat lesser mortals.

Throughout the 16th century, beds became bigger, though probably not much more comfortable than the pile of rugs or furs on the floor which had served in earlier times. But at least they were raised off the ground and roofed in, following the precedent of the northern European countries where the intense winter cold stimulated the imagination to discover ways to combat it.

Nearly all the early Tudor furniture which has survived is made of oak, but one should not assume that no other wood was used for furniture. For instance, the *Household Expenses of the Princess Elizabeth* (edited in 1853 by P. C. S. Smythe) show a payment of forty-four shillings and ninepence for 1551/1552 'to him that made her grace a table of walnut tree'. Though thrifty, the young Princess had an income of £3,000 per annum and it is hardly likely that she chose walnut because she couldn't afford oak. In fact the walnut was almost certainly imported, and therefore more expensive, as English walnut with its uneven grain, has never been much good for furniture. To form an even grain the tree must grow the same amount each year, and in England the weather is never the same two years running.

In the days when transport was difficult it is obvious that most joiners used whatever wood was most easily available – oak, beech, ash, elm, according to what grew near where they worked, in the same way that builders of houses used local materials whether brick, stone or cob. Even today common-sense does sometimes override fashion – and how much more it did then.

CHAPTER FOUR

# 1550-1600. *The Age of Exuberance*

THE hundred years from about 1550 to about 1650 covers a steadily progressive development of furniture, both in variety and style. The first fifty years showed an ever-increasing desire for display, an exuberance which reached its zenith about 1600. Thereafter the style of furniture gradually became more restrained and more refined until it more or less petered out in the long dark days of the Commonwealth. The style can be traced, therefore, rather conveniently for the student, as rising to a peak midway through the period and declining thereafter.

The rise is nearly enough contemporary with the reign of Queen Elizabeth I (1558-1603), a time when wealth was increasing rapidly and equally rapidly changing hands. The noble families who had had Church lands dished out to them after Henry VIII's Dissolution of the Monasteries were busily building mansions for themselves, as were the members of the rising merchant class. It was an age of expansion when great fortunes could be speedily made, and were often as not speedily lost. The age of Drake and Raleigh, of Shakespeare and Ben Jonson, of the Cecils and Philip Sidney, of poets, pirates and politicians, with no very clear dividing lines between the three.

In this time of bubbling exuberance domestic architecture flourished and blossomed, and furniture flourished and blossomed with it. Houses had become homes and the country was internally at peace. No longer need a householder fear that his home would be pillaged by an armed band of his neighbours, so it was no longer imprudent but was indeed fashionable to furnish the house lavishly. The peace might be disturbed by external events, the beacon fires which warned of the coming of the Armada lighted the multi-paned windows of many a splendid new house, but, on the whole, the Englishman felt secure in peace and prosperity.

However, with the closing of the monasteries the main source of artistic inspiration had been cut off abruptly. The English had only a very sketchy idea of what the Italian Renaissance was all about, and what idea they did have filtered through from France or Holland in a garbled form. The Elizabethans never really grasped the fundamental principles of classical architecture and when they applied the classical orders to their buildings or their furniture they got them all wrong. For example, the very magnificent beds of the period often employed a classical capital to the bedposts. But the column which supported it would suddenly sprout a great round blob of carved wood in the middle. The fact that the order is based on strict mathematical proportions – ratios between circumference and height, and so forth – passed them by completely.

Nevertheless, Elizabethan furniture, though lacking in grace, is solid, well-made, skilfully carved and, by any standards, imposing.

Oak would be for a long time yet the most favoured wood although of course less important furniture was made from whatever indigenous wood happened to be handy, just as houses were built of stone or of brick according to the local availability.

When attempting to date furniture of the Elizabethan period two somewhat conflicting factors have to be borne in mind. Firstly, only a small proportion of the population could read and write and roads were almost non-existent. Even the streets of London were only strewn with gravel. Secondly, the total population of England and Wales was very small, it was not until the end of the next century that it topped the five million mark.

The result was that the rich and powerful – the people who built houses and ordered furniture for them – were concentrated in the seat of power which was the Court. There weren't many of them, and mostly they knew one another and could see what everybody else in their little circle was doing. Therefore there was a great uniformity in the furniture they had made for their new houses. Against this was the fact that many of their estates were in remote districts and all the furniture was made by local craftsmen who could only rely on hearsay or on sketches which their patrons drew for them. Some patrons were undoubtedly very good at it, but they cannot all have been. The wonder is not that the surviving furniture of the period is so different, it is that it is so much the same. They triumphantly overcame the difficulties of communication, both mental and physical. It just shows that those few who were educated, were highly educated. As for the submerged tenth – though it was more likely the submerged nine-tenths – they couldn't afford much furniture anyway and what there was must have been very crude. But this is speculation, and idle speculation at that, because none of it has survived.

One can, therefore, watch the main stream of development and notice the changes in fashion as they occurred. But this is not to say that one can with any confidence clap a precise date on anything. What one can certainly say is that such-and-such a piece is typical of a certain period. And that, I am afraid, will have to do. In fact it is quite possible that it was made many years later. The joiner might have been an old man, set in his ways, who reproduced the fashion of his youth. Or he may have been avid to make something in the latest fashion and had only just heard what that fashion was, possibly ten or twenty years after everybody else.

Let us, then, consider the furniture of a house typical of the well-to-do in the Elizabethan period, and next see how it would have changed in the years leading up to the Civil War.

The great hall was still the most important room but it was no longer the only one. People had begun to appreciate privacy, and although the word 'family' would, for the next couple of hundred years, signify the whole household rather than only those related to its head, there was now a distinction between the served and the servants. An Elizabethan hall was a place where the head of the household dined together with his wife and children – and any guests there happened to be – but the servants ate in their own quarters. The main meal of the day was taken in daylight. (In William the Conqueror's time it had been about nine o'clock in the morning and gradually over the next nine hundred years it moved onwards a full twelve hours.) Father and mother sat side by side and they alone had chairs, everybody else sitting on stools. Even a hundred years later Charles II, while in exile declined the chair he was offered when dining with a French Duke and insisted on taking a mere stool. It was not only an example of his beautiful manners, it was the custom of his country.

The dining table of Elizabethan times was set in the centre of the room, instead of against the wall as previously. This was because the fire had now been moved to one wall and most, if not all, its smoke went harmlessly up a chimney. People sat all round the table, as we do today, and without the wall to lean against they were made more comfortable by having backs to their stools. But there was a great social distinction between these 'backed stools' and proper chairs which had arms.

The table was a magnificent affair. Still, at this period, rectangular, it was no longer designed to be moved about and, being of solid oak was very heavy. Four or six sturdy legs supported the top and they in turn were strengthened by rails running from one to the other. These rails, called 'stretchers' were only a few inches from the ground and were no doubt convenient for putting your feet on, thus escaping some of the draughts which swept through these huge ill-heated rooms. The legs of the table had great bulbous excrescences halfway up. The descriptive modern term is 'melon-bulb' and they do indeed resemble a melon cut in half and joined together with a plain ring in the middle. The halves have raised ribs, narrow where they join the leg and widest in the middle where they meet the ring, just like a melon.

It has been suggested that this melon-bulb may be symbolic of the Cup and Cover of the Eucharist, similarly to the linenfold motif on panels which may have represented the Napkin.

While I am perfectly prepared to accept this theory, I cannot help thinking that it is probably just a shape which the Elizabethans happened to like. You see it in portraits of the Tudor period where the men wear those funny short sleeves, slashed so that the contrasting colour of the inner material shows through, pinched into ribs like those on melon-bulb table legs. These 'puffed' sleeves must have been so remarkably inconvenient that I can only suppose that men tolerated them because they were the height of fashion.

The legs of tables were not joined directly to the top but to a frieze which, in the finer examples, is carved. This carving usually takes the form of a *guilloche,* circles interlacing like the centre of a figure eight and repeating down the length of the frieze. Enclosed in these circles is a formal design, either like the spokes of a wheel or perhaps, in the most elaborate ones, a Tudor rose.

The Elizabethans invented a clever way of making their tables larger when occasion demanded. This is known as the 'draw-leaf' table and is very ingenious. Beneath the top are two leaves which can be pulled out so that the table is doubled in length. The original top then drops down and rests on extensions projecting from the leaves, so that the whole thing is level. Also the weight of the central top pressing on the projections of the leaves keeps them stable. Succeeding generations have tried all sorts of ways of extending tables but nobody has ever found a neater method than the Elizabethans.

During this period, chairs – what few there were – became lighter in weight, presumably because they often wanted to move them from the table to the fireside. Instead of consisting of an enclosed box, or little chest, with the hinged lid forming the seat of the chair, they now became pieces of furniture with a single purpose – for sitting on. The box bottom was done away with and legs were substituted. Another type of chair was a folding X-shape. Italian in origin, it must have been very convenient for taking from one room to another or even from one house to another. But the result of all this moving about was that these chairs soon got broken and few of them survive.

But whatever shape Elizabethan chairs took they were un-comfortable. In fact the only place where an Elizabethan could enjoy some comfort was in bed, and consequently whenever they wanted to take the weight off their feet they popped into bed. The magnificence of these beds reflects their importance. A typical one would have an elaborately carved headboard with roundheaded arches to the panels. At the foot two mas-sive posts supported the roof or tester. The frame was quite plain with holes bored along its sides and ends through which webbing or rope was stretched. The mattress was not unlike a Victorian featherbed, that is a sack stuffed with feathers or wool. Blankets were made of fine wool and in the very grandest houses the sheets were of silk. From the tester were suspended curtains, usually of linen sometimes embroidered with coloured wools. When not in use these curtains were pulled back against the posts, but they were secured at the top and did not slide on rings or rails.

These beds took up a lot of space and formed a sort of room within a room – very snug and cosy. Modern man is the only animal which likes to sleep with as much fresh air as possible – the Elizabethans, like dogs and cats, didn't worry about that, and their beds were designed to keep out as much fresh air as possible. Even two hundred years later the appren-tice to the sculptor Joseph Nollekens considered that his master was quite, quite mad to sleep with a window open.

Lesser folk, such as a poor relation acting as bodyservant, would sleep on simple truckle beds.

A surprisingly large number of chests have come down to us from Elizabethan times, which suggests that they had a lot of them – in bedrooms as well as in halls or 'solars' – those nice little sitting rooms above the porch. The chest had changed little from earlier in the 16th century. The construc-tion was still the same and so, often, was the linenfold motif of the decoration of the front panels. However the medallion-like roundels of *Romayne* work went out of fashion. Some-times these chests would be made with a little lidded-box high up on the side just under the lid. These are often called 'salt-boxes' but I very much doubt if they were really made for

43

holding salt. Salt was expensive and the Elizabethans loved highly flavoured food but it seems improbable that they kept it in a place where it would all too easily get into their clothes and blankets. It is much more likely that they used these little boxes for jewellery or any small items which would otherwise work their way to the bottom of the chest.

The Elizabethans also loved colour and they couldn't have too much of it. Bare walls would be covered with tapestry if they could afford it, or with painted linen or plaster if they couldn't, as well as with the rich golden sheen of oak panelling. In its natural state oak fades to a soft silvery grey with age. Some of the furniture of this period retains its golden colour because it was polished with beeswax, but when vegetable oils were used they have darkened with age. But in the 16th century the sun shining in through those enormous small-paned windows ('Hardwick Hall, more glass than wall') would have lighted these rooms to a mellow glow.

Against this blaze of colour a piece of furniture had to be pretty emphatic if it was to be noticed at all – and the Elizabethans wanted their furniture to be noticed. It was easy enough to throw a rug of 'Turkey-work'—in other words a carpet – over a flat surface like a table but with a cupboard the effect could only be achieved by some permanent form of decoration. The habit of painting furniture had declined, probably because it was easily chipped and also it would not stand out against the colour on the walls. That, then, left them with two alternatives. They could carve the wood or inlay it with other woods of contrasting colours.

The method of inlaying was to sketch a design – formalised flowers, vines or ivy usually – gouge the wood out to a depth of about a quarter of an inch and then cut the contrasting wood to fit. It was a laborious and highly skilled process so that, not unnaturally, it is found only on the very finest furniture of the period. For the contrasting wood they used only those with a very close grain like box or holly and, if expense was absolutely no object at all, ebony and ivory. A simpler, and extremely effective arrangement was to alternate light and dark wood in rectangles or squares like a chessboard.

1.
The ornate and vigorous carving of this massive bed of the late 16th century shows the Italian Renaissance interpreted with more enthusiasm than accuracy. (Keil).

2.
This group of furniture dates from approximately the second quarter of the 17th century and shows a more restrained though no less vigorous use of carving than the bed of fifty or sixty years earlier, shown in Plate 1. (Keil).

3.
By about 1670, after the introduction of walnut, carving had become less over-powering. The wide mesh of the canework and the 'barley sugar twists' are very typical of the period. The chest-of-drawers, with its original handles, dates from the early 18th century. (Keil).

4.
Raised panels and mouldings decorate this chest-of-drawers made in the last quarter of the 16th century, and show how taste had changed since the chest in Plate 2. By the time of the chest-of-drawers shown in Plate 3, the grain of the wood was allowed to speak for itself, with almost no further ornamentation. The deep second drawer and the bun (or 'pad') feet appear on furniture of this period whether made of walnut (as in this example) or oak. (Spink).

5.
By about 1690 chair backs had become higher and narrower and the mesh of the canework finer. Made of beech painted black and gilt, these chairs have their original velvet-covered loose cushions. (Spink).

6.
The ornamental 'X' stretcher, the turned legs and the arched apron are very typical of tables of *c.* 1960. (Wrey).

7.
A fall-front walnut cabinet inlaid with floral marquetry, with a drawer in the frieze of the twist-legged stand. This type of marquetry was introduced from Holland soon after 1660 and continued into the 18th century. The stand of this fine specimen indicates a date *c*. 1690-1700. (Hotspur).

8.
Arabesque or sea - weed marquetry was introduced a little later than the floral type, but did not supersede it. This very early example of a bureau dates from the last years of the 17th century. (Keil).

Unfortunately for the collector, Elizabethan furniture seldom comes on the market nowadays. Inevitably it has become scarce and most of what remains has found its way into museums. However, enough remains in the great houses for which it was made, like Hardwick Hall (1591-1597) for us to be able to see it in its original setting. In fact it is the great houses where there has been a continuity of family ownership which offer the student of furniture the easiest lessons. While each succeeding generation added to or replaced the old furniture according to the taste of the time, the most resplendent pieces were always respected, however old-fashioned they might seem. This undoubtedly gives us a distorted view of Elizabethan furniture. It can't all have been as marvellous as the little we can see today, but, while we are sad that so much humble furniture has been lost to us, let us be thankful that we can still look at, if not buy, the very best of the period.

# CHAPTER FIVE

# *1600-1650. A Time of Uncertainty*

THE furniture style of the second half of the 16th century and the first half of the 17th century can be likened to a car which accelerates to maximum speed and then coasts to a standstill. It was still going flat out when the 17th century opened and its own momentum carried it on for some thirty years until the clouds of the Civil War slowed it down, and it finally ground to a halt at mid-century when the austere Puritan regime of the Commonwealth actively discouraged any show of splendour.

It was, of course, a continuous process, and while there is all the difference in the world between the elaborate, gaudy furniture of the last days of Queen Elizabeth and the bleak utilitarian stuff which was produced when Oliver Cromwell was dictator, it is far more difficult to trace the subtle changes in the half century after the Queen's death. It is not really very helpful to try to label furniture 'Jacobean' or 'Carolean' and to establish a dividing line between the two. While it is possible to establish a difference between the two extremes of style, the intervening changes were a gradual development rather than an abrupt change of taste and fashion. In any case, the Courts of the Stuart kings did not have as much direct influence on the styles as had the Tudors. This was not because they did not exert as much power but simply because there was a rising middle class who had money but not the entrée to the Court.

Also, of course, if you are going to use the terms 'Jacobean' and 'Carolean' you have to remember that James I reigned from 1603 to 1625 when he was succeeded by Charles I who died on the scaffold in 1649. However, as the Civil War had been raging for seven years before Charles's execution, I find it hard to believe that many people concerned themselves with the making of fine furniture then. They were far too busy fighting, fleeing, or simply trying to live quietly and escape notice. There is nothing like a war – and particularly in the country over which it is fought – for causing the fine arts to wither. The point of view changes diametrically; from being something to show off to your friends, furniture's value becomes its suitability for barring the door against your enemies.

But all this lay in the future in 1603, and for that matter in 1625. Furniture was being produced in greater quantities than ever before and it gradually became more refined and more comfortable. Let us not confuse the issue by trying to divide it into 'Jacobean' and 'Carolean' but, except where we can date it precisely, let us call it 'early 17th century'. People who use the terms 'Jacobean' and 'Carolean' get into a fearful muddle when they want to talk about late 17th century furniture made in the reigns of Charles II and James II. You can, of course, call Charles II furniture 'Caroline' as long as you are sure that whoever you are talking to understands what you mean. But with James II it is even more difficult. 'Jacobite' means something quite different and as far as I am aware nobody ever says 'Jacobine'. 'Jamesian' might do, but that has been pre-empted by Henry James. So shall we settle for 'early 17th century' to cover James I and Charles I, and 'late 17th century' for Charles II and James II?

In fact it is more appropriate to use the rather general term 'early 17th century' because of the difficulty of dating the furniture of the first two reigns exactly. Without newspapers, radio, or television, no new style can possibly have spread quickly and uniformly over the whole country, and as many of the people who were now commissioning good furniture never went to London they cannot have known the latest fashions. The squire furnishing his new manor house in, say, the remote parts of Cornwall or Northumberland was no doubt perfectly content with something which his cousin, living

47

in London would have considered hopelessly out of date.

Nevertheless, new ideas did gradually percolate, and a very good example of the way things changed over the years leading up to the Civil War is the melon-bulb form of carving. I have already drawn attention to its resemblance to the puffed sleeves of Tudor times. As sleeves grew longer, ultimately to be gathered at the wrist, so the melon-bulb gradually became elongated until finally the ribs disappeared altogether and it became a smooth cylinder much smaller in diameter, and the only trace of its origin was a turned ring near the top. In table-legs it was transformed into a baluster and on the upper tier of cupboards the lower three-quarters were dispensed with altogether, leaving a small vestigial knob hanging down from the top like a stalactite. It was as if the furniture maker had said 'This is a melon-bulb. You all know what a melon-bulb looks like so I needn't bother to carve one.'

But if the melon-bulb fell from favour, other traditional motifs for carving did not, and the linenfold flourished until the middle of the century. In fact it is a strange thing about carving that however inventive the carvers were in the lay-out they tended to use the same motifs over and over again. The arrangement and the proportions varied widely but they all drew their inspiration from the same vocabulary of motifs, and a pretty limited vocabulary at that. Roundels with a geometrical design in the middle, which may well have been a highly stylised form of the Tudor rose, *guilloches,* designs scooped out, tall narrow round-headed arches and known as 'flutes' all appear on a very great deal of the furniture of this period. So, too, does another form of arch in which no wood is scooped out, but two parallel lines are cut to suggest the form of an arch.

Other familiar, though less common, devices are trees which take the form of espaliered fruit-trees as drawn by a child, vine leaves, occasionally even a bunch of grapes and, rarely, an ear of wheat. A man with a chisel in his hand can seldom resist attacking a plain surface, and these designs are usually interspersed with squiggly lines and dots.

A very decorative form of carving which is often found on

the fronts of cupboards or chests of this period is 'strapwork', so-called because it looks exactly as if leather straps had been laid in a pattern over the surface. It was quite easy to do – simply a matter of gouging out the surrounding wood to leave a flat surface, slightly raised. You see the same idea on the elaborate ceilings of the period, except that in ceilings the strapwork is generally punctuated with pendant knobs. But the strapwork of furniture is better executed because the carver could take his time. The man doing the ceiling, however, had to work at great speed to finish before the plaster dried. (A different and better method was developed in the 18th century when the plaster would be carved in sheets and afterwards attached to the ceiling, but in the 17th century the plasterers carved *in situ*.)

The fairly crude inlay of the period was confined to the grander furniture, but there was no inhibition about mixing it with carving on the same piece. In the latter part of the 17th century it was never mixed.

Chests continued much as before, as indeed they were to until early in the next century when they finally gave place to chests-of-drawers (though even then they lingered on as strictly utilitarian articles made of pine). The chests of the early 17th century were of oak, with their frontal panels decorated with applied arches or linenfold panelling in the case of the fine furniture. The more run-of-the-mill ones had plain panels with, at most, a simple frieze of one of the standard motifs above. A typical example would have a frieze of *lunettes,* a range of semi-circles filled with a tree of a geometrical design and interspersed with squiggly lines. But a new development was to insert a drawer in the base of the chest, the genesis of the chest-of-drawers. It cannot have been very satisfactory, as it is almost as much trouble to bend down and pull out a heavy drawer as it is to rummage about at the bottom of a chest.

A more sensible piece of furniture is that which is often – and often erroneously – called a 'bible box'. These were actually small portable chests, very useful for holding papers. The ones with sloping tops were convenient, when placed on a table, for use as a writing desk or for propping a book on.

Beds remained basically unchanged except that the posts were more slender and the curtains were decorated with 'crewel-work', wool embroidery on linen.

Tables, too, did not change much except for the way in which the legs, like the bedposts, became thinner and shaped like a baluster. The drawleaf was still frequently made and the shape remained rectangular. The major development was a smaller – that is not a dining – table with an extra flap. Not, however, on the drawleaf principle, but hinged. When folded it hung down at the side of the table and when raised it was supported on a leg which swung out. This is such a good idea that it has been used ever since.

From this was developed a full-sized dining table with a flap along each of its long sides. Its ends were slightly curved so that when it was open it formed an oval, almost a circle. I have reluctantly to admit that I do not know when this sort of table – called 'gate-leg' because the supports swing like a gate and look not unlike one – first appeared. It was certainly popular in the second half of the 17th century and probably the first ones were made in the 1620s or '30s. It remained in fashion until about 1730 when mahogany, a much stronger wood than oak, permitted tables to be made with thinner legs more widely spaced. For it must be admitted that a gate-leg table has an awful lot of legs which are highly resistant to human ones. Also it has the disadvantage that when the flaps are down you cannot push a dining chair under it. Not that that would have worried our 17th century ancestors because their habit was to push the chairs, and stools, back against the wall, a habit which was to persist for another two hundred years.

Although chairs were still regarded as status (or should it be situs) symbols, they were becoming more general, and the early 17th century shows several distinct types. The heavy oak chair – direct descendent of the panelled box-type or early Tudor times – was massive and sturdy. The front legs, usually of baluster shape were firmly positioned by a stretcher only just clear of the floor. The back legs were plain and as the chair was designed to stand against the wall there was no reason why they should not be. Similarly, the panel which formed the back was deeply carved with very little plain surface on the front. In contrast, the back of the panel was completely plain. This tradition of an ornamental front and a plain back persisted long after the fashion of pushing chairs back against the wall when not in use was abandoned. Even as late as Victorian times, when the centre of a room was so cluttered with furniture that you almost needed a map to get from one end to the other it was still the fronts, not the backs, of chairs which were decorated.

The heavy oak chairs of the early 17th century had good solid arms and the top rail frequently extended beyond the width of the back panel. It was often topped with a scroll cresting and the angle between the ends of the top rail and the uprights of the panel was filled in with scrolls. The back was set at an angle so that you did not have to sit bolt upright and the back legs were splayed towards the rear to prevent the whole thing from toppling over backwards. The tilt of the back undoubtedly made these chairs more comfortable than their straight-backed predecessors but it was not until the end of the century that somebody noticed that the human spine is curved and shaped chairs accordingly.

It was in the early years of the 17th century that turning, which had been known for a long time, suddenly became fashionable and, like all new fashions, it was rather overdone. A straight piece of wood was turned on a primitive lathe operated by a treadle and, certainly in country districts, the return spring was formed by a young sapling. The resultant turnery took the form of a series of bobbles, rather like a lot of ping-pong balls threaded on a string with washers in between them. This 'bobbin' turning was used for legs of furniture and a special type of (to my eye hideous) chair was invented to show it off. This chair was triangular, with two legs in the front and a single one at the back. Arms, legs and stretchers were all bobbin turned and only the three-cornered seat was left plain. It must have been as uncomfortable as it was ugly. Fortunately such chairs are extremely rare today.

Fashion in clothes always has an effect on fashion in furniture, and whenever hooped skirts come in chairs are made to accommodate them. The first example happened in the early 17th century with the introduction of the hooped 'farthingale' skirt. Obviously a woman wearing this voluminous garment could not be squeezed into an ordinary chair, so a special farthingale chair had to be created. It was considerably lighter in weight and it had no arms so that the skirt could spread sideways. The seat was not a board, but was upholstered. Webbing straps, as used in beds, were padded with wool and covered with velvet or needlework, with, possibly, a silk fringe to hide the nails. The back was also thinly upholstered and the base of the back panel was raised clear of the seat. The seat itself was somewhat higher off the ground than in the all-wooden arm chairs.

The concession to comfort of soft upholstery was not confined to the farthingale type of chair. A refinement of the folding chair of the previous century was the treatment of the old frame. No longer capable of being folded, it was an elegant and comfortable piece of furniture with a deep cushion shaped to fit over the soft seat. These cushions were, in the finest examples, stuffed with swansdown and covered with silk or velvet. A delightful property of swansdown is its resilience, when you get up from sitting on a swansdown cushion it quite quickly regains its original shape, so that it never needs shaking. A very fine example of one of these upholstered X-frame chairs is now in the Victoria and Albert Museum. It belonged to Archbishop Juxon who attended King Charles I at his trial and lived on to place the Crown on the head of Charles II.

While the characteristic English style of furniture had emerged in the 16th century as a result of the disruption of Italian influences following Henry VIII's split with Rome, by the early years of the 17th century it was showing considerable signs of approaching nearer to that made in the rest of Europe, though it would still take another fifty or sixty years to catch up completely. The skill was already there, but the knowledge was not. That highly civilised man, King Charles I, formed a magnificent collection of paintings, and he was an enthusiastic supporter of the genius Inigo Jones, the first Englishman to study in depth and apply the lessons of the Italian Renaissance. But although carving became more restrained and classical motifs such as pillars began to be applied to furniture, the average Englishman still had only a dim idea of the classical proportions. If matters had taken a different turn, by the middle of the 17th century English furniture would very probably have been as fine as anything made in Italy or in Louis XIV's France. But they didn't. As the clouds of the Civil War gathered on the horizon interest in furniture not unnaturally waned and when the clouds burst it must have ceased altogether.

In the twenty years from 1640 what little furniture was made was as bleak and austere as the times themselves. Carving disappeared altogether (though turning carried on) and the rich silks and velvets gave place to leather. The only worthwhile style to emerge was a dining chair, lower than a 'farthingale' and with its leather back and seats held in place with nails with big round brass heads. At a time when the Puritans were busily going round chopping the noses off statues in churches and England was staggering under a highly efficient police state it is small wonder that only the very few who were rich and powerful enough to defy Cromwell's dictatorship were able to build houses and furnish them.

Indeed, the style of furniture which had prevailed early in the 17th century would have ended abruptly if it had not been for the Pilgrim Fathers who took it with them to America. Those determined – and surely rather grim – colonisers manfully faced a tremendous challenge. They applied the skills of their mother country to the entirely different conditions and the rare pieces of furniture which survive are a testimony both to their skill and their determination. They were soon building houses as well-constructed as any they had left behind them, and, spurred on by the necessity for survival, they invented a system of central heating which had not existed in England since Roman times and was not to be equalled for over three hundred years.

They did not know about, and would not have dreamed of copying if they had, the elaborate furniture of the courts of the first Stuart kings. But they did copy the sensible, middle-class furniture which they had grown up with, and well into the late 17th century excellent furniture was being made in America in a style which had been fashionable in England fifty or sixty years before.

But it was not only a furniture style which the Americans preserved; they took with them, and have maintained ever since, the spelling of certain English words, such as 'honor' and 'humor' which were the accepted form when the *Mayflower* sailed, and there is one word, 'skillet' which is still current in America and has almost passed from contemporary English. Originally a skillet was a three-legged cooking pot, designed for standing in the embers of a fire. They were heavy things, and the handle had to be long enough to be grasped by both hands. Skillets made during the Commonwealth add a curious footnote to social history. The ringing of church bells was prohibited by the stern Puritan regime and as a result no new bells were made. The wretched bell-founders, with their livelihood cut off, turned their skills to more mundane purposes, one of which was the making of these cooking pots, as their descendants continued to do well into the 18th century.

They brought to the humble skillet not only their great crafts-manship but also the fine bell-metal (approximately one quarter tin to three quarters copper) and they moulded their initials or a motto on the surface of the long handle. 'Ye* wages of sin is death' has a particularly Puritan ring about it, but some of the bolder bell-founders indulged in a little subversive Royalist propaganda. 'Loyal to His Magiste' was a favourite one, and I have seen it preceded by the injunction 'see you be' with the words abbreviated to the letters C.U.B. Not very witty, perhaps, but even after three hundred years it can still raise a slight smile, and a smile in gloomy Puritan England was certainly worth its weight in bell-metal.

---

*'Ye' was pronounced 'the'

# CHAPTER SIX

# *1650-1700. 'A Merry Mood.'*
## *The Introduction of Walnut*

'ALL the world in a merry mood, because of the King's coming' noted Samuel Pepys* in his diary, on the return of Charles II from exile. The state of euphoria did not last long but it ushered in forty years of progress at a rate which had never been known in England before. The furniture of the period shows an advance which is almost bewildering in its rapidity. Tentative new ideas became general practice in an incredibly short time. To find a parallel one has to come forward three hundred years to compare the first forty years development in aviation, radio, and the motor car.

Hitherto the spread of new trends had been leisurely, but now everything happened at once. In the stagnation and austerity of the Commonwealth people had gone without so much for so long that, with the Restoration of King Charles II, they were determined to make up for lost time.

But, as so often happens, the means did not match the will. Paying the enormous standing army of Cromwell's time, together with the distrust of foreign countries for the regime, had brought England to the edge of bankruptcy. Until the Treasury could be replenished there was no question of any grandiose schemes. The first thing was to expand trade and Charles and his advisers set about this with zeal and vigour. They realised that it is an economic fact of life that you cannot have exports without imports, and the flow of exotic goods to this country had a big influence on the furniture made here.

*One of his descendants told me that he had no reason to believe that the name had ever been pronounced anything other than 'Peppis'.

They had just got the economy on to its feet when it received two staggering setbacks. In 1665 London was ravaged by the Plague and in the next year the Great Fire swept away the warrens of timber-framed houses, and with them the rats which had brought and spread the disease. Within a fortnight, what John Evelyn described as 'that miracle of a youth, Mr Christopher Wren' had prepared a complete plan for a new London. Because of the vested interests involved the phoenix arose in a much modified form, but it was still a phoenix. A new London sprang into being and if it did not have the wide boulevards and splendid vistas which Wren envisaged, at least it housed the citizens, and housed them in considerable comfort. There was not the money – or the time – to build great mansions but the small houses were more comfortable, more convenient, and more solidly constructed than their predecessors. When one of them caught on fire Pepys noticed with approval that the burning roof timbers fell inwards so that the fire was contained within the one brick building and did not spread to adjacent houses.

These London houses – and the similar ones built in the country – had great charm. Panels became large, often consisting of three boards instead of one, and with height in proportion. Towards the end of the period fireplaces were often sited across a corner which gave the small rooms an intimate cosy appearance. Such rooms cried out for small items of furniture and the larger pieces were designed to be seen close to. The delicacy of walnut veneers and marquetry loses its impact if it is viewed from a distance.

Charles II and his Court had spent their exile in France and Holland and when they returned they brought with them the fashions of those countries. The King had the agreeable habit of making himself available to receive any subject who had been loyal to his father or who had helped him in his own escape after the battle of Worcester. It became the fashion for the country gentry to spend the winters in London which, by the end of the century, had a population more than ten times as great as any other city in England. Consequently a great many people were able to copy the styles which they had seen at Court, or which their friends had, and so the new fashions spread all over the country in a very few years.

While the roads were still muddy tracks a primitive form of postal service had begun and special furniture was developed for the convenience of letter-writing. Towards the end of the period tea-drinking became fashionable. Not popular, because tea was very expensive, but distinctly fashionable and this, too, gave rise to specially-designed tea-tables, as well as to the dainty little cups – at first without handles – out of which it was drunk.

Venice had long been the world centre of glass-making, but the high cost of its importation to England had kept Venetian glass extremely rare. However, as early as 1570 glass was made in England by processes similar to the Venetian, and by the reign of Charles II it had become a flourishing and important industry. Large sheets of mirror-glass were produced and these needed frames which gave the furniture makers a wonderful opportunity to display their prowess. (Before the invention of mirror-glass they used polished metal.)

There was a 'break-through' in clock-making and the highest skills were employed in fashioning suitable cases for these novelties.

With the increase in literacy book-cases began to appear, and Samuel Pepys had a particularly fine one made with doors with glass panes.

Cabinet-making became a craft on its own – chair-makers for chairs, and tables still being made by joiners – and no sooner was a new style introduced than somebody thought of a way of improving it. So it was in 'good King Charles's golden days' and it is doubtful if there was any recession in the making of furniture during the short reign of James II. The Revocation of the Edict of Nantes in 1685 resulted in many Huguenots fleeing from religious persecution and taking refuge in England where they set up workshops to produce the fine silk and needlework which provided rich upholstery.

Furniture making in general received a fresh impetus with the arrival of King William III and Queen Mary. In Holland they lived in one of the most lovely small palaces in Europe, built for them by the Dutch people. Naturally they were not prepared to put up with anything less agreeable and the building of Kensington Palace and the refurbishing of Hampton Court provide more lasting monuments to them than even the great military genius of William III. Queen Mary is reputed to have introduced to England the attractive blue and white earthenware which had been made at Delft since the early 14th century and is still being made there today. They brought with them, or were soon followed by, a number of highly-gifted craftsmen and designers of whom the most famous was Daniel (or Daniele) Marot, a Frenchman who had worked for Louis XIV before moving to Holland to become William of Orange's chief cabinet-maker.

So, when the century ended forty years after the Restoration of Charles II, the art of English furniture had risen from the dull, pedestrian stuff of the Cromwellian period to be on a par with any in the world.

Of all the innovations and improvements probably the one which must have contributed most to the convenience of the average household was the general use of furniture with drawers. Drawers were not a new invention but previously they had been rare in English furniture. From having a single drawer at the bottom of the chest with a great cavernous compartment above, the joiners started making chests-of-drawers almost as they have been made ever since. Almost, but not quite. The early chests-of-drawers had two shallow drawers side by side at the top, then came a deep full-width one, and two more shallow (but full-width ones) below it. This arrangement of having the heaviest drawer where it can be most easily got at strikes me as being by far the most sensible arrangement, and it is surprising that this fashion did not continue. Probably something which had a lot to do with its demise was that these big drawers, when full, were very awkward to pull out. They rested on the carcase and had no runners to ease their action.

A few chests-of-drawers were made during the Commonwealth and the ones made early in the Restoration period follow them fairly closely. They looked, and were, massive, and they were generally made of oak. They stood on short feet, round or oval and known 'bun feet'. The drawer fronts were decorated in simple geometrical patterns – squares, rectangles or diamonds, formed from raised mouldings. Sometimes, as on the cupboards made at the beginning of the century, the chests-of-drawers had lozenges stuck on them which were actually sections of bobbin-turning sliced down the middle. Handles were pear-shaped and secured by a flat strip of metal looped through a slot and fastened with tiny nails to the interior of the drawer. This gave a slight spring effect. The bottoms of the drawers were made of boards with the grain running from back to front, rather than from side to side.

The older type of top-opening chest still persisted although the better ones had the same type of geometrical raised decoration as the new-style chests-of-drawers.

Beds changed considerably, both in construction and appearance. The head instead of forming a sort of wall extending right up to the top, was a deeply-carved scrolled affair, rising in the centre to some two feet above the pillows. That was the only wood visible. Everything else was covered with velvet and embellished with gadrooning and fringes of gold or silver thread. The frieze was very elaborate and was sometimes surmounted with scroll ornaments covered in silver or gold gesso, or even plumes of real ostrich feathers.

Obviously these beds were exceedingly costly and only the very rich could afford them. More modest folk emulated them as far as they could, using more prosaic materials. Certainly it was not one of the very grand ones which Samuel Pepys occupied at an inn when he wrote 'Up, finding our beds good, but lousy; which made us merry'. Extraordinary sense of humour the man must have had.

For many years walnut had been used extensively on the Continent and, while not unknown in England, it was not until the Restoration period that it became popular. In the early days it slowly overtook oak as the fashionable wood and by the end of the 17th century it was considered very old-fashioned to have anything other than walnut as the main wood for furniture making. English walnut, with its erratic growth rate due to the uncertain climate, did not make very good timber. Besides, walnut trees were no more common here then than they are now. Consequently walnut for English furniture-making was imported from the Continent, from Spain, and Italy, and best of all, from the area around Grenoble in France. It was all the same variety – *Juglans regia* – but that from the borders of the Mediterranean was darker in colour and therefore lacked the liveliness of grain of the inland wood.

Walnut is much easier to carve than oak. It doesn't splinter so readily and the pulpy bits between the veins are harder than in oak, and less likely to shrink or swell. Its only drawback is that it is susceptible to worm, which must have been a great problem in the days before mineral oils.

It was, for instance, ideal for chairs. So, too, was another import, this time from farther afield. A brisk trade was developed with the Far East and one of the things brought back was bamboo cane. This could be woven into chair seats and backs and it had two advantages. It was lighter in weight and it had a slight resilience so that not only were chairs easier to move but they were also more comfortable. The side pieces of the back were turned, but not in the old 'bobbin' style. A refinement in the turner's equipment allowed him to turn a straight piece of wood into the shape of rope. This was quickly succeeded by the 'barley-sugar twist' and an added expertise was even to pierce the 'barley-sugar' vertically. The tops of the side-supports were crowned with finals and the top rail was scrolled elaborately. The front legs often ended in a form called the 'Braganza' or 'Spanish' foot. Charles II had married Catherine of Braganza and this was a fashion which had been brought from her native Portugal. However, it was only twenty years since Portugal had gained independence from Spain and this type of foot was made throughout the Peninsula, so either name is correct. The foot swells out and tucks under, rather in the shape that one's wrist would assume if one laid the back of one's hand on a table and straightened one's arm upright.

The shape of chairs went through three distinct phases in the period between 1660 and 1700. Having made that dogmatic assertion I hastily attempt to cover myself by pointing out that I am referring only to the height of fashion. I have not the slightest doubt that in remote country districts there were men who were still making chairs in a style they had learned from their fathers or perhaps their grandfathers. But, in the main stream of development, there were these three distinct phases. The first was one in which the back panel of canework was almost square and the mesh large. Next – about 1680 or 1685 – the whole chair became smaller and lighter and the back higher and narrower. The third phase was when the canework, instead of being set in a panel, extended to the full width of the chair back and the mesh became much finer. The cane was supported by a central splat.

Fairly early on in the period the form of the stretcher changed from the very low one of previous times which was simply four pieces of wood joining the legs at right-angles. The two side pieces remained in the same position but higher, to meet the ankle of the Braganza foot. The back member was moved forward so that the three formed an 'H' section. The front rail became divorced from the other three and, set higher still, it was deeply carved in scroll form.

Another type of work which underwent distinct changes in a short period of forty years was marquetry. It was a Dutch fashion and it called for enormous skill and patience as a description of its manufacture will show. The method was to take a number of thin sheets of different woods – say box, holly and walnut to name but three of the many sorts used. These sheets were then laid one on top of another with paper in between. Two thicker slices were then laid above and below and these were of some less highly prized wood such as deal. The sandwich was clamped together and on top was placed the design to be cut out, drawn on paper. With immensely painstaking care the carver would set to work with a fine saw and a steady hand.

When he had finished carving he would throw away the 'bread' of the sandwich and the three – or more – slices of the filling would each have the design cut out exactly the same. Taking the walnut as the background he could then fit in the cut-out pieces from either of the other two.

In this way a sort of jigsaw puzzle of different kinds of wood could be built up. The combinations were almost endless and sometimes a light wood like holly would be dyed pale green to simulate leaves, and ivory would be introduced in the very best pieces to make a realistic white flower. The Dutch had brought marquetry to a very fine art and their flower and leaf designs in wood are almost as naturalistic as the still-lifes in paint of the Dutch Old Masters. It is fun to identify the various flowers among which are nearly always carnations and parrot tulips whose feathery outlines display superbly the skill of the hand which held the saw.

This early form of marquetry was used in round, oblong or oval panels with a thin border of 'stringing', light-coloured box-wood cut into short narrow strips and laid round the marquetry, like a row of matches end to end.

The panels were let into the tops of small tables, and formed the decoration of chests-of-drawers, and the doors of cabinets.

A background decoration which makes an effective foil for floral marquetry is 'oyster shell parquetry'. The difference between parquetry and marquetry being that whereas marquetry is a pattern made up of different woods fitted together, parquetry is slices of one kind of wood laid side by side. The wood used for parquetry was laburnum. When cut across the grain the rings can be seen very clearly and it looks like a slice of Swiss roll. If the saw is slanted back to cut obliquely the resultant oval will have the rings of the grain close together at one end and more widely spaced at the other. It is from this appearance that this parquetry gets the name of 'oyster shell'. Both rounds and ovals were used as background to the floral marquetry panels, and occasionally one sees a cabinet or a chest-of-drawers veneered all over with parquetry.

In the last fifteen or so years of the 17th century another form of marquetry was introduced, again from Holland. This is seaweed – or, more elegantly – arabesque marquetry and it consists of only two varieties of wood, instead of the many used in the floral type. The light background is of walnut, and the darker contrasting wood which forms the pattern is either holly or box, artificially coloured. The feathery designs are very intricate and represent the acanthus leaf.

Arabesque marquetry is particularly effective on long-case clocks. As with floral marquetry, it needs to be seen close to if one is to appreciate the almost incredible delicacy of the crafts-manship.

Because arabesque marquetry was introduced later than floral marquetry, it is generally held to have superseded it. But this is not so. The two types continued to be made side by side, and one often sees seaweed marquetry on a piece which has the features of 1690 or thereabouts and floral marquetry on some-thing which bears evidence of having been made thirty years later. The patterns, both floral and seaweed, continued unaltered, only the construction of the carcase to which they were fitted changed with new developments.

So much furniture which contained drawers was being made in the second half of the 17th century that something had to be done to make the drawers slide more easily. There are few things more annoying than a drawer which sticks, and irritation was the mother of invention. A highly satisfactory, if rather cumbersome method was evolved. A block of hardwood was fitted to the carcase about halfway up the drawer opening, and a groove was cut in the side of the drawer. So that when the drawer was opened it slid smoothly with the groove running along the fixed block. A further advantage was that the groove could end at exactly the right place to act as a stop to prevent the drawer being slid back too far. To make a nice neat job they fitted a half-round beading to the carcase, to outline the drawer. There is always a tendency to improve by embellishing, so it is not surprising to find that very soon they were making this beading, inside of a single half-round, a double or even a treble one.

One of the first fruits of Charles II's policy of expanding overseas trade was the importation of Oriental lacquer. In those days the lacquer from Japan was considered the best, but later generations valued the Chinese more highly. In fact it seems to me to be a matter of personal preference as both are exquisite. Well over two hundred years later the Empress Dowager of China presented the last Turkish Sultan, Abdul Hamid, with a perfectly glorious lacquered cabinet, and she chose a Japanese one. I never expect to see a more wonderful and exquisite piece of lacquered furniture.

'Lac' is a resinous gum which hardens like metal, and to build up a surface of the highest polish the Chinese used up to eighteen coats of it, allowing six weeks for each coat to dry. The raised figures often incorporated gold and silver and the whole effect was absolutely breath-taking to 17th century Englishmen. Unfortunately, Oriental cabinet-making had not reached the perfection of English work, so the richest and most fashionable Englishmen had carcases constructed at home and sent them to the East to be lacquered. When one considers the long journey of a sailing ship battling round the Cape of Good Hope and the length of time required to complete the lacquer it is obvious that patience was a virtue of the late 17th century. But Oriental lacquer was worth waiting for.

It always seems strange to me that the English, who never mixed marquetry with carving, had no such inhibitions when it came to lacquer cabinets. These glorious and delicate pieces were mounted – in England – on stands which could not have been more elaborately and deeply carved. To my eye, they look remarkably incongruous. And, not content with carving the stands, they then plated them with silver or occasionally gold. I suppose they thought that as they had paid a lot of money for this exotic Oriental cabinet they had better give it the flashiest and most ostentatious stand that could be devised.

But they did not put the metal direct on to the wood. For one thing, it would not stick. For another, they could incise the carving more finely if they used 'gesso'. Gesso, a mixture of pure chalk and size, was made into a paste and coated on the wood. Like the lacquer, it had to be allowed to dry between coats. When it was dry and rubbed down it was hard and smooth, like ivory, and it would accept much more precise carving than any wood. Finally it was silvered or gilded with thin leaf and the raised parts were burnished. Later, in the 18th century when they used gold gesso as a base for a marble table it looked marvellous. But it clashed horribly with the delicate ornamentation of the lacquer which was on an entirely different scale.

The English were thrilled by lacquer and it was not long before the cabinet-makers found a way of reducing both cost and delay – by making it themselves. They were skilled in their own fields and they were confident that they could assimilate the Oriental techniques. All they lacked, if I may put it that way, was lac. As substitutes they used various sorts of varnish and while they may have been all right then they haven't stood the test of time. English lacquer – and for that matter, Swiss, although the Swiss later became adept at copying Chinese wallpapers – has faded and dulled, whereas Orinetal lacquer maintains its pristine brightness and looks as if it is still wet. Another way of telling the difference is that Oriental lacquer is nearly always based on black, rarely on red, but European lacquer may be cream, blue or, most commonly, green. The Europeans sometimes essayed red but it is never as bright a scarlet as the Oriental.

The gesso stands were always mated with lacquer cabinets, never with marquetry ones. These had turned walnut and the barley-sugar twist gradually gave way to what is known as the 'inverted cup'. It looks like a mushroom and may even be a vestigial descendant of the Elizabethan melon-bulb. Unfortunately such stands are now rare. The necks of the legs were very thin, and it is an inalienable habit of the human race to overload drawers. Consequently, after hundreds of years of abuse, many of the stands gave up the unequal struggle and snapped off. Those which survive are usually the ones with shorter legs with a frieze above which often contains a drawer. A cowardly evasion of replacing a broken stand is to support the truncated cabinet or chest on several ball feet. It looks clumsy and like all furniture that looks wrong, it is wrong.

The handles of drawers went through certain changes in the forty years under review but whatever shape they assumed they were all secured to the drawer in the same way – by a thin strip of metal looped round the top of the handle and passing through a single hole in the drawer face, to be anchored behind. The peardrop handle gradually became flatter and splayed out at the end to form a convenient fingerhold. An alternative form was a ring, and this is most often found on drawers in a cabinet where the peardrop would prevent the doors closing completely. These cabinets sometimes were made with a drawer in the cornice – with a convex front. When there was no drawer the cornice would be concave with steps of increasing width surmounting it.

On the Oriental lacquer cabinets there were no cornices, unless the maker of the stand decided to fit a gesso one to match it. However, they did have extremely elaborate chased and pierced metal plates round the locks, and it seems likely to me that these probably inspired the escutcheons which, also chased and pierced, surrounded the locks and formed the backplates to handles on English furniture in the last quarter of the 17th century.

In the early days of the Restoration period walnut was used in the solid, but soon veneering was introduced and quickly became so popular that by the end of the century almost all walnut furniture was made in this way. Walnut was always an expensive wood and veneering, besides being lovely to look at, was economical of this costly timber. Much cheaper wood, plain deal, could be used for the carcase, although the bottoms and sides of drawers were made of oak.

Veneer is cut across the grain and as it is never more than a quarter of an inch thick (later it was to be cut thinner still) so two adjacent panels can have almost exactly the same pattern which, with the lively figuring of walnut, was highly effective. A decorative band of a lighter wood was often used to outline the edges.

In France André Charles Boulle (often spelt Buhl), cabinet-maker to Louis XIV, invented a form of veneering using tortoise-shell inlaid in brass but this style was never widely copied until it was revived in the 19th century. As far as England was concerned, the use of tortoiseshell was almost entirely confined to the frames of looking-glasses, clock-cases, and small boxes. It was the reddish tortoiseshell which was considered the best, not the blond which is more valuable today.

Another form of decoration for mirror frames and boxes was a strictly amateur one. The young ladies of the Restoration period embroidered in raised work (since Victorian times it has generally been called stump-work). This consisted of figures – people, animals, trees and so forth – stuffed with thick cords or string so that they stood out from the background material, and sewn over with gold and silver thread. The pictures were usually Biblical and nearly always incorporated the leopard of Braganza, Queen Catherine's crest. Although most of this raised work was done in the reign of Charles II, the clothes of Moses, Abraham or whatever Biblical figure is portrayed are in the style prevalent in the time of Charles I. The only explanation I can offer for this is that the young ladies – teenagers still in the schoolroom – thought it silly to depict the Prophets in modern dress, so they used the oldest fashions they knew, those of their fathers and grandfathers. Sometimes the pictures were simply intended as ornaments and framed and hung on the walls like samplers, but more often they covered the small dressing-cases of the day. (Prince Rupert had a beauty.)

In America the colonists of New England were still clinging to the styles which had obtained in the mother country at the beginning of the 17th century, but by the last years of the century there was a flourishing trade with Europe and while it is unlikely that much furniture crossed the Atlantic the new ideas did. Consequently the latest English styles soon spread to America, at least as far as run-of-the-mill furniture is concerned. There was, however, a wider choice of timber and they no doubt used whichever came most easily to hand – maple, pine, birch, oak and, in Virginia, walnut.

German, Swiss, Dutch and Scandinavian settlers in the New World all took with them the styles of their homelands but it was not until the middle of the 18th century that all these influences combined to produce a distinctively American style.

Meanwhile, in England, furniture styles were rapidly leading up to to a Golden Age.

# CHAPTER SEVEN

# 1700-1725. The Golden Age of Walnut

WHEN the 18th century opened what is often called 'The Age of Walnut' was in full flood. It was far and away the most popular wood for furniture, and the art of veneering had reached a very high level of expertise.

Almost the whole of Queen Anne's reign (1702-1714) was taken up with the War of the Spanish Succession but the Duke of Marlborough's resounding victories on the Continent of Europe ensured that England was never in danger of invasion and the vast majority of Englishmen slept securely in their beautiful beds. 18th century wars were far less total than they have since become – strictly the affairs of the military – and they did not have much effect on the civilian population. As regards furniture, the war meant that it was difficult to get walnut from France but there was an alternative source of supply from the forests of Virginia. This *Juglans nigra* is a much darker wood than the European *Juglans regia* and has an almost purplish tinge. It was, of course, still possible to obtain walnut from Spain and Holland, but another factor added to the difficulties of importing it from France. The French walnut trees suffered sadly from the exceptionally severe winter of 1709, the hardships of which brought France to the verge of starvation are most graphically described by Sir Winston Churchill in his great *Life of Marlborough*. By 1720 the shortage of walnut was so acute that the French Government banned its export altogether.

Walnut imported into England was naturally more expensive than indigenous woods and it was always used sparingly. The carcases of chests-of-drawers and cabinet furniture were made of deal and drawers were lined with oak or ash. Chairs, certainly in country districts, were often made of the native beech – as they still are, near the Chiltern beechwoods – and stained or painted, 'Japanned'. Yew, the churchyard wood which likes chalky soils, had been unemployed since the musket had replaced the bow but now it was found to be suitable for veneering. There is not much figure to its grain, but its warm reddish colour is attractive.

Oak was by now very definitely unfashionable except for large tables. Anybody who has ever had the misfortune to put something hot down on a veneered table and seen the hideous results as the glue melts, will understand that solid oak is much more suitable for something which was to bear the full brunt of 18th century gourmandising.

But for the small tea-tables (though they were no doubt often used for chocolate and coffee, both of which were less expensive) subjected to a less harsh treatment, walnut veneer was ideal. A perfect forest of little tables had appeared by Queen Anne's time. There were the tea-tables, often made with a miniature wall or fence round the edge of the top and with veneer on all sides because they were designed to stand in the middle of a room, games-tables with a folding top and a leg which swung out to support it and dressing tables which, being made to stand against a wall, were decorated only on the visible surfaces. The games-tables would have velvet, or less commonly needlework, let into the tops if they were intended for cards or inlaid chessboards or tric-trac (backgammon) boards.

Dressing tables usually had three drawers, a wide shallow one in the middle of the frontal frieze and two deeper ones – about as high as they were wide – on either side. This arrangement meant that one could sit down and tuck one's knees under the frieze. The mirror was not attached to the dressing table, but stood on top of it on its own stand with little drawers beneath, their front curving out gracefully and the sides of the frame were attached to pillars by screws so that they could swing.

The use of screws in furniture had appeared about 1690 and during the next thirty years it became almost universal. 'Almost' because furniture outside the main stream of development –

that made by village craftsmen or estate carpenters – continued to employ the older methods of construction. For instance, the cruder way of nailing the sides of drawers to the fronts was common practice in 'Country-made furniture' throughout the 18th century and indeed right up to the time of mass-production in Victorian times. But from about 1700 – or a little before – screws were used to secure hinges.

Not that screws were ever used in drawers. Instead of nailing, on the better pieces of furniture they used a 'dovetail' joint. Fanshaped pieces were cut out of the sides and fronts of a drawer and interlocked at right-angles. In some drawers, one sees that a nail was driven through obliquely to make it even more secure. However, it was soon found that the end-cut of the side piece – which was, of course, cut across the grain – would not accept veneer as readily as the smooth surface of the front which ran with the grain. The answer, which was adopted about 1690, was to 'lop' the joint. That is to say, the dovetails of the front were the same as before but those on the sidepieces were shorter and fitted into slots in the frontpiece, rather than going straight through.

A little later than this change in drawer construction came a new type of foot for the kinds of furniture which contained drawers. This is the 'bracket' foot, so called because if you look at a pair of them you will see that their curved inner edges are in the shape of brackets enclosing the space between. Along the sides of furniture having bracket feet in the front the pattern is repeated so that the outer edges of the brackets meet at right-angles.

For a chest-of-drawers bracket feet became customary in the early years of the 18th century, as they did for the 'chest-on-chest' or tallboy. The proportions of these tallboys were very carefully worked out, and although they did not yet assume an architectural style the hand which designed them owed as much to architecture as to cabinet-making. A typical walnut-veneered tallboy has bracket feet with an apron fashioned in sweeping gentle curves between them. Above this comes a projecting 'ovolo' or curving lip moulding. This moulding is repeated above the lower chest portion but as the top chest is narrower the moulding is wider, although it projects no farther than the bottom one. The cornice consists of concave curves spreading out to form the flat top which is either veneered or left plain, depending on the overall height of the tallboy. A great deal of thought must have gone into the design because these carefully contrived mouldings have the effect of removing any suggestion of massiveness or slab-frontedness from what could so easily be a dull and clumsy expanse of timber. An added air of elegance and lightness is bestowed by outlining the drawers with herring-bone inlay let into the veneer. The herring-bone or arrowhead effect is achieved by sawing diagonally across a cube of wood and then slicing the resultant piece lengthwise, and fitting the two pieces together so that the lines of the grain slant across to meet in a point at the middle.

Two distinct types of furniture for writing had appeared in the late 17th century. The old box with a slanting top which opened to form a shelf now had a stand of its own with the fashionable turned legs. This type continued well into the first half of the 18th century. Another type was the fall-front *escritoire* (anglicised to scrutoire). This was similar in outline to the cabinet but instead of having two opening doors it had one, hinged at the bottom and supported, when open, by chains on either side. It would either have a stand, with drawers in the frieze, or the bottom half of a chest-of-drawers. It was an elegant piece of furniture when the front was closed but it must have looked an awful mess when the front was open and the shelf covered with papers. The solution to this problem was to develop the slant-topped writing table into the bureau. Besides the little cupboards and pigeonhole there is a quite large empty space so that one can thankfully shut the thing up with the papers inside it, and thus hide all the messes and muddles.

The next development, which began about the last decade of the 17th century and continued to be popular throughout the 18th, was the bureau bookcase. A very elegant piece of furniture, it had a bookcase standing on top of the bureau. The two doors would have either a mirror or clear glass with the tops rounded to form arches. Alternatively the doors might be veneered like the rest of the piece or, yet again, the whole thing might be lacquered but in that case the doors would usually have glass fronts. Generally, instead of the straight cornice which sur-mounted tallboys, bureau-bookcases had two arches, repeating those of the glass and resembling Dutch gables.

These bureaux and bureau-bookcases were made to a very high standard and it seems likely that they graced fashionable and grand houses. From the amount of furniture made specially for writing one would think that people in the late 17th and early 18th centuries spent most of their time in correspondence. In fact, I suspect that the major use for this lovely piece of furniture was to pen invitations to the many parties, balls, and social gatherings. The sheet of thick paper would be folded, sealed with wax, and sent round by the hand of a footman. Later on, the main task of a footman was to wait at table, under the butler, but in those days they were used to run errands as well as to travel on the coaches so that they could jump down and open the doors. Then there were the 'running footmen' athletic young men whose job was to run on ahead and warn innkeepers of the approach of their masters. They could far outstrip the lumbering coaches bumping along the rutted tracks, but it was a hard life and a short one. Most of them, I believe, died of pneumonia before they were thirty. However, a relic of the running footman makes an interesting collector's item. They each carried a staff, as long as a shepherd's crook, with a covered metal cup – usually of silver – at the tip. Its function was to hold a hard-boiled egg.

It was not until the early 19th century that there was any improvement in the roads, when Macadam introduced his system of metalling them. So, throughout the 18th century, the delivery of mail, was a slow, erratic business. In the decade following 1730 there were only three posts a week for Edinburgh out of London, and on one occasion the total mail consisted of just one letter (addressed to a banker named Ramsay, in Edin-burgh.) It would seem, therefore, that the beautiful bureaux of the period were not often used for correspondence with dis-tant cities.

A feature of furniture in the first half of the 18th century was the cabriole leg. It takes its name from a French ballet term which is also used at the Spanish Riding School in Vienna, and is derived from the Latin *capra,* a goat. The carbriole leg had made a tentative appearance on chairs towards the end of the 17th century, like a shy young actress making her first entrance on to a stage which she would eventually dominate. But the early cabriole legs bore little relation to the raised knee and pointed toe of a ballet dancer, still less to the front legs of a prancing horse. Almost straight, they were strengthened by a stretcher which gave them an awkward, clumsy appearance. This was particularly unfortunate because the stretchers of the late 17th century had been rather grand affairs. Both tables and chairs had X-shaped stretchers, each end joined to a leg, and at the centre of the X was a diamond-shaped platform often with a finial like a pineapple on it. The plainer stretchers which supported the early cabriole legs were much less attractive.

However, by 1710 or thereabouts, the cabriole leg had developed into its full beauty, with a boldly swelling knee and a slender ankle above a pad foot. Soon a Chinese motif was adopted, a finely-carved dragon's claw clasping a ball. The early ball-and-claw feet were realistically carved – if you can call a dragon realistic. Certainly it was a most convincing claw, and, looking at it, you feel that if it belonged to a real dragon – or say a real eagle – if the claw were raised the ball would be carried with it. By the middle of the century the claw had become more lightly carved and looks like a lizard's foot resting gently on the ball. It is rather the same story as the Elizabethan melon-bulb which started big and emphatic and dwindled away to almost nothing. The knees of cabriole legs were often carved with an acanthus leaf.

Cabriole legs were fitted to tables, chairs, the stands of cabinets, writing tables, everything which needed a leg was given a cabriole. Even our old friend the top-opening chest received a new lease of life by being mounted on a low stand with stumpy, curving cabrioles. And very handsome it looked, veneered or lacquered, or even coated with gesso, carved in low relief and gilded.

The cabriole leg was carved out of a single piece of wood and, with its two curves, was wasteful of timber. But the stresses of the double curve were such that it could carry a prodigious weight unaided, so that more wood was saved by not making a stretcher than was wasted by fashioning a cabriole.

The chairmakers of the early 18th century were quick to appreciate the engineering qualities of the cabriole leg, just as their customers were quick to appreciate its aesthetic qualities. Chairs, in fact, underwent a dramatic change at this time. Above the cabriole legs was a seat into which the cushion dropped, rather than the earlier method of overstuffing. The curves of the cabriole were echoed in the graceful lines of the hooped back. Canework was done away with and the single vase-shaped central splat was wide and strong. Also, a great concession to comfort was made by shaping the back to the curves of the human spine. Even greater comfort was provided by fully upholstered high-backed chairs with deep seat cushions and wings to shield the occupants from draughts.

But the short – though glorious – age of Walnut was about to be absorbed in the Age of Mahogany. Walnut would never quite be abandoned, but it was destined to play a minor part in future productions of English furniture. The heyday was over. But what fun it was while it lasted.

# CHAPTER EIGHT

# *1725-1750. The Introduction of Mahogany*

THE French ban on the export of walnut in 1720 meant that the most fashionable wood for English furniture was in very short supply. True, the forests of Virginia had an almost unlimited amount but getting it across the Atlantic was expensive and on top of that there was the import duty. Something had to be done, and Parliament acted with rare and exemplary speed. In 1721 they passed an Act which abolished the duty on any timber imported from any British plantation in America.

But there still, of course, remained the cost of freight and if timber had to be brought across the Atlantic why only walnut? Another wood – mahogany – had been known since the days of Christopher Columbus but the cost of bringing it from the West Indies had made its importation uneconomic when walnut was readily available in Europe. Now, however, all that had changed, and the Age of Mahogany began. At first it was only a trickle – imports in 1721 valued only £276. But by the middle of the 18th century mahogany was generally accepted as the most usual, as well as the most desirable, timber for fine furniture. By the year 1800 the value of the import was running at nearly £80,000.

This does not mean that even at the height of the period mahogany was the only wood used. Oak was still used in country districts, though in the better furniture it was confined to the linings of drawers. Some excellent walnut furniture was produced, and, of course, deal was extensively used for carcases and as a basis for gesso, lacquer and for all 'japanning' – a term which covered anything from lacquer to fairly mundane

75

paint, and, right into the 20th century the shinily enamelled tin trays and trunks.

Mahogany had the enormous advantage of being impervious to worm. Any wormholes you find in mahogany are those made by a worm taking a short cut from one piece of soft timber to another. But it had other qualities as well. The trees were huge so that even large table tops could be made from a single piece. It is immensely strong and therefore it could be carved into delicate shapes such as the 'ribbon-back' chairs associated with the name of Thomas Chippendale. Towards the end of the century it lent itself ideally to the fashion for legs so slender that it seems impossible that they could support a table top, let alone anything on it.

At first, as with walnut, mahogany was used in the solid but then, again as with walnut, it produced beautiful veneers. The earliest imports were from Jamaica, or smuggled via Jamaica from the neighbouring islands not under British control. This was a very dark wood without much figure and by about 1750 it had given place to mahogany from Cuba. Although the same species *Swietenia mahogani* – it was lighter in colour, a rich brown, like a Havana cigar. It produced lively veneers and it was generally easier to work. After the middle of the century the vast majority of mahogany came from Honduras. This was a different variety – *Swietenia macrophylla* – and is the only mahogany which has a reddish tinge. That it was not, initially at any rate, valued as highly as the Cuban wood is shown by the fact that sometimes Cuban mahogany was veneered on to it. However, during the latter part of the 18th and the whole of the 19th century it was the only variety in common use.

These three types (two varieties) of mahogany were, and still often are, lumped together under the name of 'Spanish mahogany'. This derives from the Spanish American possessions, mahogany is not grown in Europe. Not the least admirable of mahogany's qualities is its durability, and the fact that so much 18th century furniture survives today is due as much to the material as to the workmanship, outstanding though it was. It is fortunate that the best wood coincided with the highest skills which British cabinet-makers ever reached.

9.
A tallboy or 'chest-on-chest' of about 1710-1720. The careful grading of the proportions of the cornices and drawer sizes together with the lively grain of the walnut veneers avoid any appearance of clumsiness in this substantial piece of furniture. It has had no less than three sets of handles but the present set resembles the original. In a private collection.

10.
Walnut at its best. A bureau - bookcase of the first quarter of the 18th century, with slides for candles beneath the doors panelled with mirror glass. The glass would amplify the meagre candlelight. (Hotspur).

11.
The solid splat, the drop-in seat, the sturdy cabriole legs with the claw firmly grasping the ball, the shells on the knees are all typical of walnut chairs *c.* 1730. But the very effective eagle's heads are a rarity. (Phillips).

12.
Similar in style to the chair shown in Plate 11, this wing chair also has shells on the knees of its cabriole legs and strongly carved ball - and - claw feet, but it is an early example of mahogany. The 'wings' were for keeping out the draughts and the loose cushion was stuffed with swansdown. *c.* 1730 - 1740. (Hotspur).

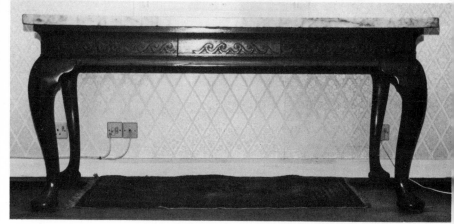

13.

The marble top of this mid-18th century side-table is six feet long and 2 feet 10½ inches wide. It takes four men to lift the top alone, and yet, such is the strength of Cuban mahogany, that the 'ankles' of the legs narrow down to a diameter of 7¼ inches. The 'wave pattern' moulding has been chipped from the face of the flush-fitting drawer. Fifty years ago this table was so little regarded that it was painted white and relegated to a kitchen. The paint was stripped by the present private owner.

14.

An illustration from the 1762 edition of Thomas Chippendale's *The Gentleman and Cabinet Makers' Director*, with suggestions for variation of decoration. (Hotspur).

15.
A writing desk which follows so closely the design shown at Plate 14 that it can be dated with comparative accuracy within a year or two of the publication of the 1762 edition of *The Director*. (Hotspur).

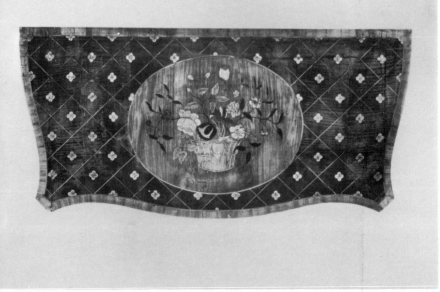

16.
The marquetry of the mid-18th century was just as naturalistic as the floral work of fifty or seventy years earlier but the designs were freer. The top of a side table. (Hotspur).

The 18th century was a golden age for cabinet-making, and the different periods justly take their names from cabinet-makers rather than monarchs. Leadership in the arts passed from the Court and was not to be regained until the coming of the Prince Regent at the end of the century. It is true that the early 18th century furniture is often called 'Queen Anne', but no doubt this is because no one great name had emerged in cabinet-making. The Queen herself, her life bedevilled by all those agonising miscarriages, had little interest in, and less influence on, the arts. George I may have influenced furniture to some extent. It certainly became rather more like the contemporary German furniture in his reign. But this, it seems to me, is more probably something which would have happened anyway. The beautiful, but often rather spindly furniture of the late 17th century had become the graceful and more robust furniture of Queen Anne's time. It appears, therefore, that logically the next step would be toward the even more robust but less graceful products of the time of George I, who has come down to us as saying in guttural tones 'I hate all boets and bainters,' so he is hardly likely to have cared much about the gentle arts in general. George II, too, cared little for the arts but George III had an ear for music and is reputed to have sketched a design for a Regimental Spode dinner service. He also commissioned some superb furniture, but he was following fashion not leading it. Probably his greatest contribution to the development of furniture is, paradoxically, the emergence of a distinct American style. After the War of Independence the Americans were anxious to throw off any ties with Britain and they made their furniture as different as they could from anything made in England.

By about 1720 there were three grades of English furniture. Firstly there was the very grand furniture made for the richest people. No expense was spared in materials or craftsmanship but the results were somewhat overpowering. These designs were magnificent but not attractive. It is awe rather than beauty that they inspire in the eye of the beholder. This grade of furniture rarely comes on the market, most of it reposing in the great houses for which it was made, or has found its way into a museum long since. The few pieces which now appear in the salerooms are beyond the reach of all but the richest collectors.

It is from the second grade, sensible, elegant, and supremely practical furniture made for the newly-risen and immensely important middle classes, that what most of what we see today comes. The third grade, that made in and for modest farms and cottages was, naturally, of simpler design and cruder workmanship. It was also made of the most easily available wood, local oak, elm which looks like oak until you get close to it and see the coarser grain, or beech. But one thing all the grades have in common is that the man who made them had a terrific pride in his work. However great the gap between Sarah Duchess of Marlborough ordering three thousand yards of damask for Blenheim Palace and the farm labourer whitewashing the walls of his cottage kitchen, they were both doing the best they could afford.

The first quarter of the 18th century was the time when the Italian Renaissance finally arrived in England. The villas which Andrea Palladio had build round Vicenza as country retreats for the rich Venetians were slavishly copied, even to the extent of having the principal rooms facing north. A wise precaution in the Veneto where the summer sun can be almost unbearably hot but not such a good idea in the cold damp English climate. The leader of this school was the third Earl of Burlington whom the waspish Alexander Pope castigated—

> Yet shall, my Lord, your just, your noble rules
> Fill half the land with Imitating-Fools;
> Who random drawings from your sheets shall take,
> And of one beauty many blunders make;
> Shall call the wind thro' long arcades to roar,
> Proud to catch cold at a Venetian door;
> Conscious they act a true Palladian part,
> And, if they starve, they starve by rules of art.

Pope need not have worried. What he left out of his reckoning was that the 'just, the noble rules' of architecture were considered to be part of a gentleman's education, and the furniture makers of the first half of the 18th century, no less than the builders, were fortunate enough to have patrons and customers who knew as much, or more, about design as they did.

In the great palatial houses the swelling lines and assymetrical curves of high Baroque found their expression in gorgeous gilded gesso. This flamboyant furniture is usually associated with the name of William Kent, the talented young Yorkshireman whose patron Lord Burlington packed him off to Italy to learn all about the Renaissance. But in fact cabinet-makers like James Moore and John Gumley were already well advanced in the style when Kent returned to England in 1719. Kent was one of the great exponents, not the originator of the style. But, versatile and brilliant though he was, Kent was primarily an architect and his furniture designs do not show any great sympathy with the material. A really fine cabinet-maker loves wood as a woman loves fur.

All the same, some of Kent's *dicta* were adopted very widely. His recommendation for 'parcel gilt' – that is the gilding of parts of furniture – was to set a fashion which lasted for many years. Even as late as the 1760s John Fowle of Uckfield in Sussex was gilding the capitals and plinths of the clockcases which he was making, not of the fashionable mahogany but of the country-man's good old standby, oak.

Simultaneously with the extravaganza of gesso eagles holding up marble table tops, there developed in the 1720s and '30s a definite architectural style of furniture to furnish the Palladian houses. Beds, for instance, would have their posts of correctly-proportioned classical columns, with the frieze above decorated with the 'breaking wave' pattern, a running scroll of capital S's joined at the base, or the 'Greek key' – like joined swastikas without one bar.

Bureau-bookcases were capped with 'broken pediments', triangles with the top angle scooped away and a platform made for a marble head or bust to stand on. The handles of all drawer furniture now generally had solid backplates, sometimes lightly engraved, but a handle more substantial than the peardrop had appeared earlier in the 18th century and by about 1720 practically all handles were secured by two fastenings. The ring was now spread out at the top, and the bottom was flatter, some-

79

times with a small ridge in the middle round which the fingers closed naturally. The perfectly good system of runner – a groove in the side of the drawer running along a projection in the carcase – was superseded by bottom runners which, in effect, prolonged the sides of the drawer downwards below the level of the drawer's floor. This has been normal construction for a drawer runner ever since, but I was delighted to find that on the 'units' in my own kitchen which were purchased in the mid-1960s the early form of projection, and, groove, fitted. And how smoothly the drawers slide!

About the time of the introduction of bottom runners they started laying the boards which form the drawer bottom sideways on, with the grain running right and left. With the back of the drawer made to stand just above the bottom the wood can expand without buckling. In the older system, with the grain running at right-angles to the drawer front, there was no room for the wood to swell and the boards therefore tended to arch up in the middle. Wood expands and contracts across the breadth, not the length, of the grain.

An advantage of bottom runners is that there is just enough space beneath the drawers to fit a strengthening strip of wood across the joints at the middle of the drawer's floor.

There was for a short time, probably not more than about thirty years from 1715 or thereabouts, a fashion for having a slightly overlapping lip on the front of drawers. Presumably because the upper projection was likely to snag on things being put into the drawer in a hurry, the makers soon modified the system. The side and bottom overlaps remained but the top was made flush with the lip moulding carved on to the solid wood of the front. It looked just the same as the other three mouldings but it had the effect of making the drawer appear more shallow from top to bottom and, if anything, rather improved the appearance. But the short-lived fashion for overlap meant that the half-round beading on the carcase framing the drawers was done away with. These are small details in themselves but they make a big difference to the look of the furniture. The flatter frontal appearance made an excellent foil to the architectural features such as pilasters on cabinets and bureau-bookcases.

By about 1730 or 1735 it became the fashion to pierce the backplates of handles. This makes them look less massive but it has the great disadvantage of making it practically impossible to clean them without getting metal polish on the wood. Personally I prefer to leave them unpolished, though this is entirely a matter of personal taste. The backplates and escutcheons may get dull but there is always a highlight on any handle used often, where the fingers hold it.

In America at this time there was a particularly happy combination of Dutch and English styles. At the beginning of the 18th century they followed the contemporary English style – which was itself, as we have seen, under strong Dutch influence. However, within the next few years a highly individual style emerged, particularly as regards the tallboy or, as it was known in America, highboy. The first deviation from the English pattern was in the turning of the legs, where the cup was inverted and lengthened to look like a trumpet. Next the cabriole leg was developed and used much more on this type of furniture than was the custom in England. Indeed, the broken pediment of the English burea-bookcase looked extremely effective when used in conjunction with cabriole legs on a highboy, and long after the English had abandoned the stand in favour of the 'chest-on-chest' construction, delightful highboys were made in America along these lines. It was a strong and vigorous style and, modified by European influences, it continued until nearly the end of the century.

# CHAPTER NINE

# *18th Century Cabinet-Makers*

IT is quite obvious why the furniture of the first years of the 18th century is called 'Queen Anne'. What is not so obvious is why the furniture of the mid-century is called 'Chippendale'. Thomas Chippendale's reputation has undergone many fluctuations in the last sixty or seventy years. From being considered the greatest English cabinet-maker of all time, his stock sank until he was thought of as little better than a charlatan. Now, however, the experts, in the light of all the evidence which has been discovered about him, have come to the conclusion that the truth lies somewhere in between. It usually does.

Thomas Chippendale was born in Otley, Yorkshire, in 1718. His father was a joiner and his grandfather was a carpenter. Nothing is known about his childhood but I like to think it was a happy one, solely on the evidence that he obviously did not rebel against his father's teaching. A year after marrying in 1748 he turned up in London. In 1753 he moved to St Martin's Lane, to cabinet-makers of the 18th century what Savile Row is to tailors of the 20th. In 1754 he published *The Gentleman and Cabinet-Maker's Director*. This was a book of designs, a sort of super catalogue. The pictures in it ranged from the fantastic to the very simple. Clearly Chippendale's intention was that anybody who wanted the furniture he illustrated should come to him to have it made, but where he was so clever was that any competent cabinet-maker could have a shot at making the easiest pieces.

This might seem rather naive but in fact it was carefully calculated. Chippendale judged, rightly, that the more famous the book became the more customers it would bring him. He did not mind humbler cabinet makers using his ideas – their customers wouldn't have come to him anyhow.

So the *The Director* was much more than a puff for Chippendale's firm. It rapidly became a textbook. A second edition was issued in 1755, containing a hundred and sixty plates and the third edition, 1762, contained two hundred. Chippendale died in 1779 and there is evidence to suggest that he contemplated a fourth edition.

Chippendale himself did not draw or even inspire the illustrations though the introduction implies that he did. Two hundred years before what its practitioners like to call the profession of public relations was established Chippendale was a pastmaster at it. The whole thing was a deliberate publicity gimmick, and a highly successful one. What cannot have been intentional was that over a couple of hundred years later the magic name of Chippendale is clapped on all furniture of his period and much of the stuff on each side of it. That is an added bonus and I hope the shade of Thomas Chippendale is chortling over it in some celestial hall of fame.

But spare a thought for the chaps who actually did the work. Matthias Lock had already published drawing books and, with his collaborator, a man called Copland, was almost certainly responsible for the great majority of the illustrations in Chippendale's book. The firm of Thomas Chippendale was undeniably an important one, but it would be absurd to suggest that all its products were the work of the head of the firm as it would be to suggest that Henry Ford built every Model T. More absurd, really, because Henry Ford probably had a great deal more to do with the design of the Tin Lizzie than Chippendale did with his furniture.

Nor, of course, was Chippendale the only large-scale maker of furniture, any more than Henry Ford was the only manufacturer of cars. William Hallett (1707-1781) was at least equally regarded and was probably even more successful. He certainly made enough money to buy the estate of the Duke of Chandos at Canons in Middlesex and to erect a fine house there. William Vile and his partner John Cobb supplied furniture to George

83

III, which Chippendale, significantly, was never asked to do.

Furniture making was big business in the 18th century and many firms, large and small, were engaged in it, as well as individual cabinet-makers. Unfortunately, the English never adopted the French custom of marking their furniture with the maker's name or sign and it is therefore seldom possible to positively identify its origin. It is rare to find bills or correspondence relating to any but the most important pieces so that the great bulk of 18th century furniture will always remain anonymous, unlike silver or pictures.

The larger firms were more like interior decorators are today and would undertake the complete furnishing of a house. They employed not only cabinet-makers, joiners, carpenters, carvers, gilders, and looking-glass framemakers but upholsterers and drapers, smiths and glass-grinders. There were also draughtsmen, designers, and journeymen, the ancestors of the commercial travellers. There must have been keen competition between these firms, and one which could produce a really attractive catalogue would have the edge over its rivals particularly where country customers were concerned.

But, before the days of photographs, it was impossible for an illustrated catalogue to give a precise idea of how the piece of furniture would look, so sometimes the furniture maker would construct a model of one of his typical products and take it for his customer to see. One occasionally sees such things as chairs in miniature labelled 'child's chair' but usually – usually, not always – it was a model to illustrate the full-sized article.

The great London furniture makers often supplied furniture to the owners of large country houses and, considering the appalling difficulties of transport, it is a wonder that it arrived safely. But it did – a great tribute to 18th century packing. (The cost of packing was a heavy item. In 1775 the three gilt stools which the cabinet-maker Thomas Ward sent to Lord Langdale in Yorkshire cost a mere £3 each, but '67 foot Packing case at 2¾d' came to 15s. 4d., and there was another shilling for 'Battens of wood etc. and packing.' The stools fetched £900 the three at auction in 1959.)

It always amazes me that our ancestors never allowed themselves to be deterred by difficulties which we – or anyway I – would think insurmountable. Without electric power, the internal combustion engine or any form of transport faster than the horse they nevertheless got things done. They built enormous houses, moved hills to improve landscapes, and provided their own entertainment. When they wanted something they got it, never mind how long it took or how much it cost. A typical example is the way they obtained ice in summer. Instead of shrugging their shoulders and giving the whole thing up, they carefully dug sunken ice-houses which they packed with blocks of ice taken from ponds or lakes, covered it with bracken or straw, and used it the following summer. With the coming of steam, great trainloads of ice – I believe two a week – would be sent from the Canadian lakes and brought across the Atlantic to provide a sorbet in the middle of the gargantuan Victorian dinners. Nothing was too much trouble provided that the man who was paying got what he wanted.

It was this spirit of demanding and getting perfection which inspired the 18th century and brought the art of furniture making to its highest peak of craftsmanship. It was a restless age, always seeking new frontiers of knowledge to cross, always questing after new experiences, avid for new ideas. It was into this atmosphere of eager expectation that Thomas Chippendale launched *The Gentleman and Cabinet-Maker's Director*.

His timing could not have been better. The book's success was immediate. 'I frankly confess,' Chippendale wrote coyly in the preface, 'that in executing many of the drawings, my pencil has but faintly copied out those images that my fancy suggested.'

This, as we now know, was not true at all. The fancy was Lock's, the pencil Copland's. But Chippendale got away with it at the time, in those far-off days before the Trades Descriptions Act. Let us hope that the impresario adequately rewarded the labourers in the vineyard. At the same time, let us not be too hard on Thomas Chippendale. His was the presiding genius, and his entrepreneurial triumph was based on a sound knowledge and experience of designing and making furniture. Above all, he gave the public what it wanted.

What made the appearance of the book so particularly apt was that people were getting tired of Palladianism. They could find no fault with it but it had ceased to thrill them. They were ready for a change, and Chippendale gave it to them. In fact he did more – he offered three separate styles – the Rococo, the 'Chinese' and the Gothick.

Rococo was not entirely new. The French had been using it for some time and in 1745 Matthias Lock had published some charming engravings of looking-glasses and wall-lights in the style. But it was while working for Chippendale that he – possibly at Chippendale's suggestion, certainly with his approval – modified the French *rocaille* taste to form an identifiable English style. Light and charming, graceful and strong, it could hardly have been more different from the ponderous architectural furniture which it superseded. Some of the designs in *The Director* are fanciful to the point of whimsy and were probably not intended to be taken too seriously. Chippendale the showman was well aware of the importance of exaggeration and over-emphasis to drive home a point. But the great service which *The Director* did to English furniture making was to show simpler styles which any competent craftsman could copy or adapt.

Rococo was the most popular of the three furniture styles of the mid-century but the other two, Chinese and Gothick had their enthusiastic following particularly amongst the intelligentsia. Not that there was anything very intellectual about 18th century chinoiserie. The designers drew freely on their lively imaginations – none of them ever went to China. The only one who did was Sir William Chambers the great architect, but all he had to do with furniture was to shake his head sadly over what was made in the name of the Chinese.

The Chinese taste, as interpreted – translated would be a better word – into English took the form of rather charming trellis work, and the concave curve of a pagoda roof. (This very individual Chinese roof form derives from the time, thousands of years ago, when this ancient civilisation was nomadic. The sweep of the pagoda is a copy, in more permanent materials, of their ancestors' tent roofs.) Another pseudo-Chinese motif was the 'Ho-ho bird' a giant creature with a long neck which perches uneasily on the top of many a mid-18th century looking glass frame.

18th century Gothic – they spelt it 'Gothick' and this form is generally used to distinguish it from the early, real Gothic – was just as fanciful as the chinoiserie, but in details much more closely related to the original. There were, after all, plenty of Gothic buildings for them to go and look at, and look at them they did. This enlightened age, with its interest in science and the general advancement of Man, nevertheless cast a nostalgic glance over its shoulder. The high priest of the Gothick cult was Horace Walpole who 'Gothicised' Strawberry Hill; 'a little plaything-houses that I got out of Mrs Chenevix's shop* and is the prettiest bauble you ever saw. It is set in enamelled meadows, with filigree hedges.' One can almost hear the shrill yelps of delight as he fashioned the tracery windows and plumped down the battlements on the top. Gothick, in short, was fun and not to be taken too seriously.

It is a tribute to the sturdy commonsense of 18th century cabinet-makers and their customers that they exercised great restraint in interpreting these styles. Horace Walpole could well have substituted Chippendale for Shakespeare when he wrote, in 1764, 'one of the greatest geniuses that ever existed, Shakespeare, undoubtedly wanted taste'. But the excesses in *The Director* were largely ignored and the cabinet and chair makers concentrated on the more sensible pieces.

In 1754, the year in which the first edition of *The Director* appeared, a young Scotsman was studying the newly discovered ruins of Herculaneum. Robert Adam was the son of a good conventional Palladian architect who had sent him to Italy to study.

Now all the architects of the 18th century had influenced furniture because the cabinet-makers designed furniture to be appropriate to the rooms in which it was to stand. Some architects, like William Kent and Henry Flitcroft, designed furniture themselves. But Robert Adam carried the whole thing much farther. He planned the entire room down to the last detail, walls, ceiling, floor, carpets, fabrics, fireplaces and grates,

*A fashionable toy shop

87

everything down to the coal shovel. If they had smoked cigarettes in those days he would have designed the ashtrays as well. To see his furniture at its best one should view it in the setting for which it was designed, such as Osterley Park or Kenwood, both very near London. Instead of the white ceilings with the heavy cornices and mouldings of Palladian houses Adam decorated his with geometrical patterns of complementary colours – pink and apple green were his favourites – divided by delicate raised plaster mouldings which were always left white. Some of his ceilings incorporate small panels of allegorical painting by Angelica Kauffmann, very different from the huge and exuberant baroque decoration by Thornhill three-quarters of a century earlier. The carpet would be woven to repeat out-lines of the pattern of the ceiling.

The whole effect was the quintessence of elegance. Stately and formal splendour for stately and formal occasions, it was all in exquisite taste but it was anything but cosy.

Adam culled his decorative motifs from the ancient civilisations of Greece and Rome as well as Renaissance Italy and he used them with unerring skill to create a style peculiarly his own. Rams' heads, honeysuckle, pendant husks, fluting, round and oval medallions, urns, all were woven into his strictly regular patterns.

But the style was so intricate, so grand, so expensive, that it was the prerogative of the very rich and fashionable, far beyond the means of the great majority of merchants and country squires who were buying more modest stuff.

However, although Adam was not widely copied his philosophy was. Gradually it came to be accepted that even quite simple furniture should have the clean lines and perfect proportions which governed Adam's ideas, and inspired the whole classical movement. How widespread it became can be judged by the fact no styles other than the classical appear in Hepplewhite's *The Cabinet Makers' and Upholsterers' Guide*.

The book was published in 1788 by George Hepplewhite's widow Alice. He himself died in 1786 but whether he died suddenly while the ink was still wet on his drawings, or whether he put the work aside when a lingering illness overtook him we shall never know. In fact very little is known about Hepplewhite the man. He is thought to have been apprenticed to Gillow of Lancaster and he certainly had a shop – or at least premises – in London at Redcross Street, Cripplegate. But it is doubtful whether any furniture was made there. If it was no record survives.

Hepplewhite's book describes the latest fashions, the fashions prevalent at the time. He is best regarded as a reporter rather than as an innovator. His book does not forecast the next style. What it does – and does brilliantly – is to tell us about the current one. Hepplewhite collected all the loose ends of the classical style and wove them into a coherent pattern.

But although there can be no question about what he did what still remains unanswered is when he did it. This poses one of those problems of detection which make the study of antiques so fascinating. Obviously Alice Hepplewhite did not consider the style to be out-of-date otherwise she would not have bothered to publish the book. Or, just supposing she did it as a sort of last tribute, it would have sunk without trace. Its great success which amounts also to immortality disposes of that possibility. We are, therefore, on safe ground in assuming that the classical style was still at the height of its popularity in 1788 and that it had achieved this popularity several years earlier. The Hepplewhite style can, in fact, be held to cover furniture made from about 1780 or even 1775 or thereabouts.

All the Adam motifs appear in Hepplewhite's drawings except the ram's head but the lines of the styles are freer and less rigid. It is quite extraordinary how much impression of movement the furniture designers of the 18th century managed to get into static things. It is only the architects – Kent, Flitcroft, Adam – who failed in this, though they achieved a great sense of movement in their buildings. Perhaps they felt more at home designing for stone than for wood.

Paradoxically, the man who had as great an influence on furniture design as any was neither an architect nor a cabinet-maker. Thomas Sheraton had been a journeyman cabinet-maker in his early years (he was born in 1751 at Stockton-on-Tees) but after he came to London he devoted himself to teaching drawing, preaching and designing furniture for others to execute. Between 1791 and 1794 he published his *Cabinet Makers' and Upholsterers' Drawing Book* in four parts. The designs are wonderful and the man was obviously a genius. Alas, like so many geniuses, he was not appreciated in time to relieve what Adam Black, a Scottish publisher who was employed for a week by Sheraton to write an article for his next book, describes as his 'painfully humble circumstances'.

Like any good 18th century author, he roundly flayed the opposition who lacked the protection of the law of libel. 'Notwitstanding,' he writes in his preface, taking a side-swipe, 'the late date of Hepplewhite's book, if we compare some of the designs, particularly the chairs, with the newest taste, we shall find that this work has already caught the decline, and perhaps in a little time will suddenly die in the disorder.'

He was too optimistic. His own designs were simply the next stage in the classical revival which was to continue well into the 19th century, and while his own designs for chairs certainly did oust Hepplewhite's the classical revival as a whole swept on with its two prophets, Hepplewhite and Sheraton, greatly honoured in their own country.

Not, however, in America. After the War of Independence, anything British was not unnaturally anathema to them. The Americans bent over backwards to be different. However, although they took their lead from the French instead of the English, it is difficult to draw a firm line because by the time of Duncan Phyfe there was so little difference between the French Directoire and the English Regency styles that it was impossible to tell which had provided the inspiration. But in the interval between the War of Independence and the emergence of Phyfe the Americans made furniture which lacked the genius which had come before and was to come after.

In the 1750s and '60s they designed and made furniture of great variety, each area producing furniture appropriate to its houses. The cities of the Eastern seaboard had small brick or stone houses, the plantation owners of the South built huge and lovely Italian-derived villas, and the New Englanders developed the wooden house (from the very early days they had, of necessity, found how to give them central heating). Each district had furniture which looked right in the houses for which it was made, an easy adaptation of the mid-18th century rococo.

But even the exquisite designs of, say, William Savery of Philadelphia, which gave an American idiom to the language of Chippendale, were replaced after the Revolution by furniture in the classical style. Unfortunately, though, this furniture, in spite of being superbly made, lacked the true spirit which made this style so superlative in England and France. In their determination to be different, the Americans did not pause to consider how best to create an individual style to replace the one they were trying to avoid. In fact their country-made pieces were much more successful, and far more representative of an emerging nation, vigorous and strong. The craftsmanship was competent and the designs forceful and original. Their Windsor chairs were to develop into the American 'rocker', one of the most distinctive types of national furniture in the world.

The roots of the classical style were in Europe, but the branches, even though they were slightly mishapen at times, were the Americans' own. On both continents the classical style, whether with a French, English, or American accent, dominated the second half of the 18th century.

# CHAPTER TEN

# 1750-1800. *The High Peak*

ENGLISH furniture of the second half of the 18th century was as fine as any made anywhere in the world at any time. The designers were knowledgable and highly skilled. The cabinet-makers fully comprehended what they were trying to do, and had the tools and the materials to do it. The customers were educated in the arts and were not satisfied with anything less than the best.

The consequence is that the finished products were of a quality of design, construction, material, and fitness for purpose that has never been equalled before or since.

When the customer said 'make me a drawer' the cabinet-maker did not have to ponder on how best to do it, he already knew and could draw on the experience of his predecessors as well as his own. Freed from the need to puzzle out the technical details, he could let his imagination roam and range over the whole field of contemporary thought. He had at his disposal a great mass of design books – Chippendale had many, many imitators – and he could pick and choose, adding embellishments or simplifications of his own.

It is possible to recognise a particular piece of furniture as being entirely in the Chippendale, Hepplewhite or Sheraton style, but it is far more likely that one will see one which owes its origin to two of them. A great connoisseur of this period once said to me, rather wistfully, 'I only seem able to find transition pieces.'

With the craftsmen skilful and inventive, and with the patrons keenly aware of current trends and yet having ideas of their own, it is not surprising that the furniture is highly personal and original. No two customers would want exactly the same thing, no cabinet-maker would want to make exactly the same thing twice. Then, again, cost came into it. The great architects of the 18th century were not above a bit of jerry-building and similarly cabinet-makers occasionally skimped materials or time to save expense. Furniture which shows signs of economy is usually called 'country-made' but I have no doubt this is a slur on many an honest craftsman and that much of it came from London workshops.

But nearly all the furniture of the second half of the 18th century is instinct with good proportion. However crude the workmanship and however humble the material it all looks attractive. Whether grand and ornate or modest and simple it has an air of distinction and even the heaviest pieces give an impression of lightness and movement.

This half century covers the greatest age of English furniture. Whereas hitherto one can trace a single line of development, in these fifty years – less than the span of two generations – so much happened so quickly that it would be wrong to think of progress as a spearhead. Rather, the great army of furniture makers was moving forward on the broadest possible front. It is, therefore, better to concentrate on the consideration of one item of furniture at a time and to see how it changed over the fifty years.

By the middle of the 18th century the stool was at last going out of fashion except as a formal decoration for a hall or passage. However, as late as 1756 John Whitby described as 'back stools' what we should call dining chairs. The tall wing chairs were probably much more common than would appear from the relatively small number of survivors. Before the days of loose covers or the Victorian anti-macassar their velvet or needlework upholstery must soon have got filthy from the men's powdered wigs which came into fashion in the reign of George I. Also these chairs were very comfortable and anything comfortable tends to get worn out quickly. It is the wooden chair with only the seat upholstered which has come down to us in quantity.

In the middle of the 18th century the cabriole leg was still flourishing, either with ball-and-claw or pad foot, at the

D

front and the back legs (nearly always with pad feet) were curved towards the rear in a slightly convex manner to give good solid support. It was in the back that the greatest difference lay between the chairs of the early and mid century. Instead of the hooped back, the top rail met uprights at rightangles. On the finer examples it is undulating and often carved. But it is with the central splat that the carvers really went to town. They exploited the potentialities of mahogany to the full, and created most elaborate splats, fashioning the wood to resemble ribbon or a series of arches in the 'Gothick' taste. Sometimes there was no central splat and the whole back would be filled with arches or trellis work in the Chinese taste. Awe-inspiring though these elaborate backs are, I must confess to a preference for the simpler styles of the 'country-made' chairs where the beauty of the wood is allowed to speak for itself.

The curve of the cabriole would have looked inappropriate with the straight lines and rightangles of the Chinese style (although the ball-and-claw was originally a genuine Chinese emblem) so a straight leg was substituted. Even though, on a heavy chair, straight legs require a stretcher to brace them against wobbling about, there is still a considerable economy of timber over the cabriole, and so the return to the straight leg was rapidly adopted. When combined with a 'Chinese' back, the stretcher would be fretted, and the front and side rails of the seat would have a matching decoration carved in the solid.

Another alternative to the central splat was the 'ladder-back', so called because the horizontal splats are reminiscent of the rungs of a ladder. This form is said to have originated in the North of England and it is interesting to compare the country-made pieces with their more sophisticated town cousins. The country ones have turned legs and rush seats and are made of elm or beech whereas the town ones are upholstered as any other chair and made of mahogany with legs following the prevailing fashion.

Robert Adam designed some chairs with solid oval backs, upholstered, the legs turned and reeded with oval medallions decorating the top of the front ones, and the front and side rails with fluted carving. Beautifully proportioned, of superb workmanship, to my eye they lack an essential characteristic of a good chair, it ought to make you want to sit in it. Adam's chairs, especially those with the back in the shape of a lyre, are the last word in elegance but they cannot be called inviting. Hepplewhite's designs – however much Sheraton may have derided them – seeem to me to have more human warmth. I certainly want to sit in them – albeit gingerly because they look more fragile than they really are. I think this is probably because the backs of most of them are constructed on a different principle from previous chairs. Instead of a central splat rising from a shoe fitted to the back rail of the seat frame Hepplewhite's designs show round, oval, or – his most famous designs – shield-shaped backs. All of these are mounted on supports which are continuations of the back legs, rising above the seats.

Hepplewhite stated 'chairs in general are made of mahogany' but there were, naturally, exceptions. Satinwood had already made its appearance and was occasionally used for chairs, though its properties were really more appropriate to the types of furniture which could display a large expanse of it. Imported from both the East and West Indies, satinwood is aptly named. That from the West Indies has an even colouring of pure pale yellow while the East Indian has an orange tinge. Both glow with a very high sheen. When used for chairs satinwood would be painted – but not in the fashion of Robert Adam. He designed furniture to be painted all over and for this it was not necessary to have a beautiful wood, beech or pine would do. But when satin wood was painted it was only with designs – flowers, ears of wheat and so forth – which stood out against the glowing background of this lovely wood.

Ears of wheat appeared, too, in carving and were favourite emblems of Hepplewhite's hoop-back chairs. This form of hoop-back was quite different from that of the walnut chairs earlier in the century, with their wide spoon-handle splats. Hepplewhite's retained the old central splat but it was pierced and its members carved with the wheat-ears, as were the fronts of the side rails which curved over in the form of a round-headed arch to form the top rail.

This sort of thing is, of course, typical of any age of transition

95

between one style and another. While Hepplewhite's shield-backs mark a distinct new fashion the origins of the hoop backs can be traced back through Chippendale to the beginning of the century. The form is entirely different but the general idea is the same. Another example of the transition period in chairs is the one which has a vase-shaped pierced splat with the suggestion of the shield about it, in the way in which its curves come together in a shaped V.

There is nothing surprising about transition – it is a natural process. One can hardly imagine a chair-maker – or a designer or cabinet-maker, come to that – suddenly tearing up all his old drawing books, forgetting the habits of a lifetime, and saying 'henceforward I will make nothing that is not in this new style'. And even if he did his customers probably would not agree. There is never a definite switching off and switching on. Rather there is a gradual merging.

Nor is any new style the last word. Every style develops as it goes along. The furniture makers of the second half of the 18th century had fine tools and materials, highly refined techniques, and considerable ingenuity. They were, therefore, well placed to make improvements between one piece of furniture and the next. For the most part it was only detail improvement, the straight front leg of a chair was very plain so, to cheer it up a bit, somebody had the idea of making it slightly serpentine in profile and finishing it off with a couple of reeded mouldings down the edge. But with the coming of more delicate backs a different form of leg was needed if the design was not to look out of proportion. So the legs were tapered with a ridge at the ankle to give what is called a spade foot.

A completely different type of chair appeared about the middle of the 18th century – the Windsor. It was in the truest sense of the words 'country-made' and it originated in the Buckinghamshire beech woods. It owed little to contemporary fashion and was to continue in basically similar form almost up to the present day. A Windsor chair is one in which all four legs are mortised into the bottom of the solid wooden seat and the supports for the arms and back are mortised into the top. Windsor chairs never, of course, became as grand as fine mahogany ones, but they were good honest farmhouse furniture and they were made in a great variety of shapes and woods. It is not uncommon to find one with beech legs, an elm seat, and yew arms.

One peculiarity of Windsor chairs is that the arms come farther forward than they do on ordinary chairs of the second half of the 18th century. They certainly help you to lift yourself out of them but they must have been constricting to the wide-skirted men's coats and the women's voluminous skirts. A typical parlour or dining room chair had its arms set well back, supported by sweeping concave curves from the seat frame at the tops of the front legs.

Before we leave the period of Hepplewhite two other types of chair must be mentioned. One has a particularly elegant back comprising three feathers – a graceful tribute to the Prince of Wales whose device it was. Hepplewhite evidently thought highly of this design (as I did myself when I saw one – perhaps the only one – made from it). In various forms the three-feather device was widely used. The other type of chair was made by most of the fashionable chairmakers from about 1765 for the next thirty years and was an almost exact copy of the current French fashion. Almost, but not quite. The English ones are less flimsy and consequently not quite so dainty. Often they were painted overall (mostly white or very pale colours) and picked out with gilding. In France they preferred to leave the wood unpainted and Marie Antoinette used to send hers to Les Invalides for the old soldiers to sit in and rub the ends of the arms with their horny hands to bring up a good polish.

A typical English one has an overstuffed (as opposed to a drop-in) seat, a padded back and padding on the arms. The satin covering is secured with ornamental brass nails.

I was once walking down St. James's Street, in London, with a friend when a superb black Rolls Royce glided to a halt beside us. 'You know,' said my friend, 'that car's in such good taste that it's almost vulgar.' I have often been reminded of that remark when admiring chairs of Hepplewhite's period. I respect them, I like them immensely, but I am inclined to shake my head and say 'Life isn't like that'.

97

Sheraton's designs bring me back to earth. Not that he couldn't be pretty ethereal himself, given good condition of wind and tide. But in the main his designs are highly practical, and highly original. Instead of the almost mincing delicacy his chairs are emphatic and what decoration there is is used to maximum effect. Dainty curves give way to straight lines but where his genius lies is in that he achieved solidity without sacrificing gracefulness and appearance of lightness. He set the fashion for a deep top rail which extended well beyond the uprights of the back. It curved concavely to fit the sitter's back. The plainness of such a wide sweep of mahogany was relieved by thin 'stringing' of a lighter wood, slim as a pencil line. I suspect that he was bending over backwards to be different because the backs of his chairs, in contrast to the elaborate designs of Adam, Chippendale and Hepplewhite, had practically no filling at all – a couple of crossed members or a single, rather wider horizontal rung. There was no carving and the legs were either straight and tapering or – and this style became more strongly emphasised after the end of the century – slightly curving, so that the leg formed an arc.

Leather was considered too crude a covering for these delicate chairs and horsehair became popular. But not the coarse black stuff which the Victorians liked. At the end of the 18th century it was usually dyed red or green, often with a black stripe, it was very soft and also hard-wearing.

During the fifty years from the middle to the end of the 18th century 'case furniture' – that is anything made with drawers or cupboards – went through a number of changes. At the beginning of the period the French style of serpentine fronts became fashionable for chests-of-drawers and it was often used to great effect on the small drawers in the enclosed parts of bureaux which were otherwise rather plain. Generally these small drawers had pigeon holes above and they flanked a small cupboard whose single doors would have pilasters on either side like the front door of a house. Nearly all these bureaux have secret drawers, some of them fairly obvious, such as when the steps leading up to the door or the pilasters flanking it pull out. But the cabinet-makers were highly ingenious and many of the secret drawers are extremely well hidden in the thickness of the carcase. They are usually made of cedarwood and although tiny they could contain a lot of golden guineas or banknotes. Until 1759 the lowest denomination of bank note was £20, when the £10 note was introduced, to be followed by the £5 note five years later. In the days when the roads were bad and footpads and highwaymen abounded a man would not lightly undertake the journey to a distant bank and a lot of money was kept in the house. A locked drawer simply invited a thief to break it open, so the secret drawers had a very practical use.

Mirror glass was going out of fashion for bureau-bookcases and was supplanted by clear glass with glazing bars which might be crowned with a chinoiserie pagoda top, or covered with tracery like a church window in the Gothick taste. When a simple pattern was used the panes tended to be rectangular rather than square as was the previous practice, and the bars were thinner, following the fashion in window glazing. The thick glazing bars of early Palladian houses were bevelled and painted white to reflect light into the room but gradually they became thinner and those on furniture followed suit. However, reflecting light is not a function of a bookcase, so nothing was lost by having thin bars.

Chinese and Gothick patterns appeared, too, on otherwise architectural pieces such as tallboys but these patterns were confined to the decoration and consisted of nothing more than a line of Gothick arches along the frieze or an applied fret of Chinoiserie trellis. Both the Greek key and the wave pattern continued to appear and the reeded moulding outlining the drawer remained unchanged. The bracket foot was sometimes pierced in the chinoiserie style, and an alternative was a fore-shortened and very solid shaped bracket, like a stumpy cabriole leg. For this massive furniture the rococo influence was usually confined to elaborate gilt handles and escutcheons.

A new type of writing table appeared – the flat-topped desk. It was supported on two pedestals containing drawers, with a space between them for the writer's legs. When these pieces of furniture were designed to stand away from the wall the backs were decorated with dummy drawers to match the front. Larger ones were made for two people to work at, 'partners' desks', and the extra space allowed for two sets of drawers at opposite sides. I have even seen one made to accommodate four people.

As the century progressed the variety of writing desks and bureaux increased and satinwood was used to form a pattern of inlay on the fall-front of bureaux, or for the fronts of drawers (no longer serpentine) inside the flap. Sheraton used a tambour or roll-top which was automatically raised when the writing shelf was pulled out. Many small writing tables were made for ladies' boudoirs.

The secretaire took the form, towards the end of the period, of a bookcase standing on a chest-of drawers. The top drawer was deep and its front was hinged to disclose a nest of drawers.

The neo-classicism of Robert Adam effectively ended the taste for rococo although the other two fashions, Chinoiserie and Gothick, survived albeit in rather different forms. As late as 1775 David Garrick was furnishing his villa at Hampton with furniture in the Chinese taste, probably made by Chippendale, and at the end of the century William Beckford was having Gothick furniture made for his preposterous Fonthill Abbey. But neither of these can be considered typical. Garrick was no more representative of the majority in his time than a film star is today, and Beckford's Fonthill was considered an elaborate – and hideously expensive – joke by his contemporaries. It was for all its magnificence, a gimcrack affair. The tower, built round the clock in shifts, at night by the light of torches, not surprisingly, fell down twice and in the surviving wing the windows are large glass panes with Gothick tracery imposed inside and out. The very small amount of furniture which remains is crudely made and clumsy. William Beckford is best remembered for his wonderful collection of books and pictures.

One might think that the end of rococo was the end of Chippendale. Not so. He was no campaigner, dying in the last ditch for his beliefs. He was happy to give the public what it wanted, and if it wanted neo-classicism, fair enough. In fact it is on the work he did for Robert Adam that his reputation rests. Perhaps the height of his prowess is displayed in his commodes.

The commode is very definitely a piece of drawing-room

furniture. It was only the Victorians, with their passion for polite euphemisms, who applied the name to pot-cupboards. The 18th century commode took its name from the French and was a small chest-of-drawers or cupboards with drawers or shelves enclosed by a pair of doors. Often the top was of marble or the reconstituted marble 'scagliola' which Adam made fashionable. The front was serpentine without outward curving corners usually embellished with fine gilt mounts. Matthew Boulton manufactured these mounts on a large scale – he is said to have employed over thirty men in his gilding department alone, but, good as they are, they never quite came up to the French 'bronzes'. However, the rest of the commode was at, its best, the equal of the French work. Commodes showed cabinet-making at its finest. Veneers and marquetry were re-introduced but instead of the arabesques of the early part of the century marquetry was now used to give an almost three-dimensional effect. Vases, urns and flowers, exquisitely fashioned, stood out against a background of satinwood. Later in the century the cabinet-makers' vocabulary was extended to include exotic woods from far-away places, ebony from the East, cedar from North America, kingwood and tulipwood from Central America, coromandel and rosewood from India, thuya and zebrawood from Africa. From England itself came all the fruitwoods, holly, box, and sycamore for contrasting marquetry.

The classical style affected beds as it did everything else. The lines became sharper and lighter and it must have been delightful to wake up and see an expanse of golden satinwood above one's head and the bedposts entwined with garlands of painted flowers. The sun would have seemed to be shining even before the curtains were drawn back. In fact a bedroom in a fashionable house in the latter half of the 18th century must have been very pleasant altogether. A chest-of-drawers, possibly bow-fronted like some of Sheraton's designs, a mahogany tallboy which might have the universal dentil moulding on the cornice and a veneer of satinwood on the frieze with a string of sharp-pointed Gothick arches applied as a moulding. The dressing table would have a top cover and skirt of sprigged muslin (which is why a plain table was used), and there would be a washstand and a pot-cupboard unless the two were incorporated in one, as happened towards the end of the century.

A piece of bedroom furniture which appeared in the middle of the 18th century is often called a wigstand. It has three short cabriole legs which support a triangular shelf, usually with a ring incised into it : three more scrolling legs rise from this shelf and support one or two drawers also triangular. Above this again three more supports, either matching those below or straight, carry a circular wooden ring made to hold a small china bowl. Above the drawers, sticking up like a pineapple, is a spherical soapbox. The name comes from the theory that the wig was placed in the bowl for powdering and that at night it stood on its block on the bottom shelf. 'Wigstand' is, I suspect, something of a misnomer, or at any rate only half the story. The soapbox indicates that the basin was used for washing, and the bottom shelf could hold a jug just as well as a wig block. The name has probably arisen to distinguish it from the other type of washstand which dates from this time. This consists of a cupboard standing on straight legs and later examples have tambour sliding doors. The top is either of marble with a narrow rim round it, or it folds out sideways in two halves to disclose a basin. The bottom of the basin is concealed by the cupboard which contains a pot. Sometimes there is a deep drawer at the bottom and the front legs are split so that it can be supported when open by the halves which are attached to it. This form is called a 'nightstand' and the pot is recessed into the drawer.

The reason why many 18th century gentlemen did not need wigstands is because they had special walk-in cupboards in which they could treat their wigs without the powder flying all over the bedroom. These powder closets, which are often to be seen in houses of the period, usually have a few bricks removed from the wall to form pigeon-holes for keeping the wigs.

Dining-rooms, too, brightened up very considerably in the second half of the 18th century. At the beginning of the period dining tables were rather dull. Just vast expanses of mahogany without any ornament. However, they soon livened up and many ingenious forms of extending them were invented. Two rectangular tables, each with end flaps, would be joined together, leaves would be inserted or there would be two semi-circular ends which could be moved away and serve as pier tables when not required to augment the dining table. The cabriole leg lasted longer on tables than it did on chairs but it was eventually replaced by straight legs, the ones which supported the flaps swinging out on pivot joints. The gate-leg, which had proved such an obstacle to so many human legs, finally died away, mourned by none.

Even more convenient was the 'pillar' dining table. This consisting of a top resting on a column supported on three, or sometimes four, fairly short legs. The number of pillars depended on the size of the table – two, three, four or even five. This arrangement solved, once and for all, the problem of getting human legs under a table, unobstructed by wooden ones and these tables are as avidly sought after today as they were when they were first invented.

In the early part of the period the side table either matched the dining table or had a marble top. (It is splendid for not staining but don't put a very hot dish on it, the dish will crack, not the marble.) But change was on the way. Robert Adam designed beautiful side tables, the frieze displaying his repertoire of classical motifs, fluted carving prominent among them, with two stands to support urns at the side. Next the stands became incorporated in the table and the sideboard was born. A further development was to enlarge the stands into drawers and cupboards, fitted with compartments for wine bottles. The urns were knife-boxes and often very finely veneered and inlaid with delicate stringing.

By the end of the century the sideboard had assumed the details of chests-of-drawers and tables, bow or D-fronted, tapered legs with spade feet or reeding, and the circular metal handles on their solid round backplates. It often had an arrangement of brass rails at the back to hold plates, and a curtain to save the wall being spattered. The whole gives us a nice sense of nostalgia, all those many-course dinners with servants to wash up, afterwards.

Tables proliferated in the mid-18th century. Tables for breakfast, tables for tea, tables for playing cards, dressing tables, pier tables, side tables, just tables. What is such fun about them is that they are small and therefore suitable for the flats and boxlike houses we live in nowadays. But it was for precisely the opposite reason that tables were made small in the 18th century. They were 'occasional' tables, and when the occasion didn't arise they were placed out of the way against the wall. An 18th century drawing room looked like a modern one cleared for a cocktail party. These huge and lofty rooms must have been terribly cold in winter; a fire, when you are facing it, may scorch your face but your back remains frozen. Consequently it was necessary to restore the circulation by taking a short walk, a stately perambulation up and down the room. Naturally they didn't want to dodge round the furniture so they ranged it neatly against the walls. (It is unfortunate that when central heating was necessary they didn't have it. Although they did not suffer in vain, central heating is very bad for furniture as the dry atmosphere causes veneers to rise and crack.)

Chinoiserie inspired the design of many small tables, possibly because of the association of ideas with tea. An applied fret on the frieze, a tiny fretted gallery round the top, straight legs sometimes strengthened by diagonal stretchers, often also fretted. Occasionally one sees the legs of clustered columns and, oddly enough this idea, taken straight out of a medieval cathedral, doesn't look incongruous.

When these Chinoiserie tables had the addition of a drawer and a shelf enclosed on three sides by a low trellis or brass wire gallery in place of a stretcher they were intended for bedroom breakfasts. (A custom which persisted well into the 19th century was to receive guests during the leisurely process of getting up, and to regale them with chocolate while they watched the maid piling up their hostess's elaborate coiffure, or the valet tying the host's cravat.) These tables often had flaps, but no unwiedly gatelegs, a support swung out on a pivot.

An immense number of tripod tables appeared shortly after

the middle of the century. I say 'shortly after' because, although it is possible that they were being made at the time, Chippendale does not show a single design for one in *The Director*. They first appeared in print in the *Universal System* which the great firm of Ince and Mayhew issued in sections between 1759 and 1763. This book was undoubtedly inspired by the success of Chippendale's but the firm was famous in its own right.

Tripods had been used as the bases for tall candle stands since the late 17th century but the tables of the mid-18th century are much lower, being of normal table height, and of course the tops are wider. The three cabriole legs, with pad, ball-and-claw, or (more rarely) dolphin feet, carry a central column. The early ones have pot-bellied columns of a straight circular column with a cup emblem near the base carved with oblique and curving fluting. The later ones have an uninterrupted column of architecturally correct proportions.

The circular top is invariably hinged so that it can be swung upright when the table is placed at the side of a room. When down the top is secured by a metal latch. A good wide and thick mahogany board, unveneered, was used for the top and in some – though not necessarily the better – examples the top was scooped away so that a raised rim was formed. This rim was scalloped, like moulded pastry and consequently this style is known as 'pie-crust'.

An additional refinement, found only on the better tables, is that the top is made to revolve as well as tilt. This is achieved by means of what is known as a 'bird-cage' which consists of a block with a hole bored in its centre for the top of the coloumn to penetrate. Four little balusters support an other block which is screwed to the understide of the table. The top block is thick because it has to incorporate the knuckle joint on which the top pivots.

Another, less common, form of occasional table stood on three legs, one at each corner of a triangle. Semi-circular flaps could be raised to form a round top and the central triangle pivotted round to support them.

Still another variation of a folding-top table is the so-called

'Pembroke'. Rectangular with a flap on each of the long sides, it has a drawer in the frieze with a dummy drawer at the other end. By the end of the 18th century Pembroke tables were often made of satinwood, with their ends slightly bowed.

There were no real 'breakthroughs' in the techniques, as opposed to the styles, of furniture making during the second half of the 18th century, for the very good reason that they knew it all already. But two minor points contribute to convenience. One is when somebody had the bright idea of putting little half-round mouldings along the rightangles of the insides of drawers and thus prevented dust collecting. The other was the development of the caster. A form of caster had been made since about 1740. It consisted of a number of leather discs threaded on to a brass axle. Leather is obviously not nearly as durable as metal and one day, probably about twenty years after, somebody suddenly thought of making the whole thing of brass. No doubt he said to himself 'I wonder why nobody thought of that before'. The early leather casters were screwed into the open end of the grain, they tended to work loose after a bit. Anyway, the all-brass casters are anchored more securely by making the end of the leg fit into a square brass cup.

At the beginning of the period American fashions more or less followed English ones, after an inevitable time lag. They did not take to either Chinoiserie or Gothick, but they produced some fine rococo work. Particularly in Philadelphia, Gostelowe, Gillingham, Randolph, and Savery were combining rococo decoration with architectural outlines, rather freer and more vigorous than the European styles on which they were based, and for their highboys they employed cabriole legs to great effect, and continued to do so for some years after they had gone out of fashion in England. A feature was the strongly ornamental pediments, with emphatic carving and fretting.

Simultaneously the country regions of America produced a great variety of Windsor chairs with a far wider range of turnery than in England.

While mahogany and walnut were used extensively for fine furniture some marvellous pieces were made in local woods – hickory, maple, cherry, and many more besides.

CHAPTER ELEVEN
# The Regency. The Age of the Extroverts

NO fashion outlasts the lifetime of its own generation. The new generation always considers the tastes of its parents to be hopelessly old-fashioned, and reacts strongly against them. And a new set of tastes comes in and flourishes until it, too, is derided by the succeeding generation. Of course, new generations are coming along all the time so the pattern of change is a gradual one. However, if at any time one looks back thirty years one will find that the prevailing taste is as different as it can be from what it was then.

Thus, if we study the style of interior decoration which Robert Adam was practising in the 1770s we are not at all surprised to find that by the early years of the 19th century a revolution in taste had taken place. Instead of the highly ornate ceilings, wall mouldings and fireplaces we find an almost clinical bareness. Only a moulded cornice to relieve the flat expanse of ceilings, walls plain from skirting to picture rail, the decoration of fireplaces confined to reeding of the marble with perhaps a simple circle to mark the corners. The classical style was still classical, but its emphasis had swung from Rome to Athens. It was the utter purity of the styles of ancient Greece which was the aim.

This worked extremely well on the exteriors of buildings – Nash's stately terraces in London, the smaller but no less elegant houses of the spas and seaside resorts, and the square or rectangular country houses. The plainness was never allowed to become dull – verandahs, balconies and railings of the most beautifully wrought iron enhanced the clean lines of the stucco.

107

But the interiors were quite another matter. The early 19th century was an extrovert age, pleasure-loving and confident. Not at all the sort of people to tolerate austerity. Consequently they filled their houses with colour and their furniture was designed to draw attention to itself.

For the first time for over a hundred years there was a Royal leader of fashion. The Prince of Wales became Regent in 1811 and King, as George IV, in 1820, but the term 'Regency' is applied to the whole period from 1800 to 1830. As early as 1784 he had started his onion-domed Pavilion at Brighton and building and furnishing was to proceed fitfully for another thirty-nine years. This Oriental phantasmagoria, originally inspired by Samuel Pepys Cockerell's Mogul mansion Sezincote in Gloucestershire, was in complete contrast to the rigid classicism which governed the superb town planning which the Regent encouraged and patronised.

This conflict between the exotic and the restrained is well illustrated by the furniture of the period, and the best pieces happily combine the imaginative genius of one school of thought with the highly educated insistence on good proportion of the other.

As a very broad generalisation, one might say that furniture became heavier and more robust as the Regency period progressed. But this can be no more than a very broad generalisation. The *papier mâché* chairs which started to come in towards the end of the period are as light and ethereal as any of Sheraton's designs at the beginning, and Sheraton's own design for a bookcase is a good deal heavier than many which were made in the 1820s.

In 1750 the total population of England and Wales was slightly under six and a half million. By the time of the census of 1801 it had risen to 8.8 million, and by 1831 it was almost fourteen million. (The population explosion is, therefore, no new thing.) With this expansion of the population went an expansion in the national economy. Not only were many new fortunes being made out of the Industrial Revolution, but money – and spending money at that – was reaching a far wider spectrum of the nation than ever before. In short, there were a

17.
With the flap shut this mid-18th century mahogany bureau is very plain, but when the flap is down very delicate decoration is revealed—pigeonholes, serpentine fronted small drawers, columns outlining the door of the central cupboard, and inlay of contrasting woods. Handles are original. In a private collection.

18.
The same, with the secret compartments open.

**19.**
Two mid-18th century circular tables, both of mahogany and with hinged tops which revolve on 'bird cages'. The one on the right has a scalloped 'pie-crust' edge. In a private collection.

**20.**
*Left* Many ingenious forms of small table date from the third quarter of the 18th century, such as this with its triangular top which turns to support the flaps when raised. Usually they had plain pad feet, like the circular tables shown in Plate 19. These elegant representations of high-heeled shoes are exceedingly rare. In a private collection. *Right* The same, with the flaps raised.

22.
Restrained use of Gothic arches and Chinoiserie frets on a chair *c*. 1760. (Hotspur).

23.
John Whitby's invoice of August 14th 1756, made out to the last Lord Langdale, refers to this chair.

'To 6 Back stooles with Carved fraimes of Mahoganey Stuffed up in Canvass all cumpt: readey for the needil work covers att 27 shillings.'

Both chairs and invoice are still in the possession of the great-great-great - granddaughter of the first owner.

**24.**
The beauty of these mid-18th century chairs lies as much in the gently sweeping curves as it does in the sparing use of carved decoration. (Hotspur).

**25.**
Shield-back chairs of 1780-1790 ornamented with the 'Prince of Wales feathers' associated with George Hepplewhite's designs. (Hotspur).

lot more people with a lot more money. They were going up in the world and they aimed to secure their new positions in society by lavish display in their own homes. The traditional patrons and customers, too, the nobility and gentry, still had unabated capital, leisure, and knowledge.

All in all, then, the furniture industry thrived mightily. Demand seemed never-ending, and supply matched it. Communications had improved vastly thanks to the system of metalled roads developed by Macadam, and new ideas spread rapidly. People travelled about the country in a way which would have been impossible twenty years before and they no longer had to have design books sent down from London – they could go and see the designs for themselves. (An example of this new mobility is that the Prince Regent could do a full day's work in London, reading and annotating Government papers, and then have a supper party in Brighton the same evening.)

The air was humming with new ideas, and they were eagerly snatched. I doubt if our insular race has ever been so open to the influence of foreign thought, and the more foreign it was the better they liked it. French, of course, in spite of the Napoleonic war. But the Far and Near East too, were combed for suggestions, as well as the ancient civilisations. In 1807 Thomas Hope produced a book of designs, not only of furniture but of complete rooms. Here is a sample.

> As the colours of this room, in compliance with the oriental taste, are everywhere very vivid, and strongly contrasted, due attention has been paid to their gradual lightening, as the eye rose from the skirting to the cornice. The tint of the sofa is deep crimson; that of the walls sky-blue; and that of the ceiling pale yellow intermixed with azure and with sea-green. Ornaments of gold, in various shades, relieve and harmonise these colours. Round the room are placed incense urns, cassolettes, flower baskets and other vehicles of natural and artificial perfumes.

Another room was designed to house 'a fine marble group executed by Mr Flaxman and representing Aurora visiting

Cephalus on mount Ida'. The theme was Night giving place
to Day, and Hope conveyed this impression by means of a
black marble fireplace, its frieze studded with gold stars. The
curtains were 'the fiery hue which fringes the clouds just before
sunrise' and were edged with black velvet. They covered the
whole wall but were draped back to reveal huge looking-
glasses.

Now, Thomas Hope was not joking. Nor was he looking
for customers. A rich and scholarly man, he had actually had
these rooms built to his own designs, and they must have
made the chaste Grecian rooms look painfully austere, however much they were jazzed up with the striped wall-paper
of the time. One of his rooms had a ceiling 'imitated from
those prevailing in Turkish palaces, consisting of a canopy
of trellice-work or reeds, tied together with ribbons. The border
and the compartments of this ceiling display foliage, flowers,
Peacock's feathers and other ornaments of a rich hue, and of
a delicate texture which, from the lightness of their weight
seem peculiarly adapted for this lofty and suspended situation.
Persian carpets cover the floor'.

I have devoted some space to quotations from Thomas
Hope's *Household Furniture and Decoration* because it demon-
strates so well the lines of thought which motivated Regency
ideas on how to furnish a house.

With the strong emphasis on gilding and on gilt mounts,
dark wood made more suitable contrasts so satinwood was
used less and less. Mahogany just as much as before, rosewood
much more. Rosewood has a clearly marked grain, the darker
parts ranging from mid-brown, through dark brown to lines
of black and in some cases the lighter part is almost as yellow
as satinwood. The exotic timbers – amboyna, zebra-wood and
the like – appear quite often, and ebony was extensively used,
occasionally in the solid in small quantities, for instance for
handles and parts of table-stands, but mainly for stringing.

Marquetry went right out of favour, except that at the end
of the period there was a revival of interest in furniture designs
of the time of Louis XIV and principally in the work of Boulle.
Consequently his very distinctive methods of combining brass

and tortoiseshell appeared again. But the Regency interpretation – which continued well into Victorian times – used a greater proportion of brass to tortoiseshell and although the lines are more sweeping the effect is blatant and massive. Regency Boulle reminds me of an old locomotive and I always expect it to give a shrill whistle and steam out of the room. To my mind a much more satisfying way of utilising brass in furniture is the delicate inlay on wood which was fashionable throughout the Regency.

Every type of furniture made in the latter half of the 18th century continued to be made in the Regency period and several more were added. The only familiar item of furniture which almost disappeared was the tallboy. For a brief period at the turn of the century tallboys had been made as single pieces, instead of the 'chest-on-chest' construction which had proved so satisfactory for so long. The solid cliff of mahogany, unrelieved by a break in outline, was a daunting affair and I am not surprised that the Regency folk turned away from it. The few tallboys which date from the early 19th century show a reversion to the earlier construction.

Possibly as a compensation for the lack of a second stage, the chest-of-drawers became higher, with a deep frieze, inlaid with brass or outlined in ebony. The feet were reminiscent of the bun or ball of a hundred years before, except that they were really very short legs, turned with a fat knob above a sturdy slightly tapered foot.

In the first years of the century handles were either circular brass knobs with a device stamped into their flat fronts or, on the larger pieces of furniture, rings which fitted into circular recesses on a solid round or oval backplates. A very common decoration for these backplates is a lion's mask. By about 1810 knobs were nearly all of wood, usually with a flat front and reeding round the rim.

Looking glasses have, in their frames, always shown the height of current furniture fashion and never more so than in the Regency. Frame-making had always been a separate craft from the days of the Restoration when the elaborate gilded and silvered carving vied with the best work of the furniture makers. In the early years of the 18th century parcel-gilt and veneered walnut frames were made from the choicest pieces of wood, and in the middle of the century the frame-makers really let themselves go with the Chinese, rococo and Gothick styles. They also made charming *girandoles* which had shelves for candles so that the light could be reflected by the glass. The Regency development of the *girandole* was circular. The glass was convex, to give the maximum reflection of light, and the frame was entirely gilt. Half balls decorated it and on top sat an eagle with a ball suspended by a chain from its beak. Usually, though not invariably, two curving arms sprout from the bottom of the frame to hold candles. Another very typical Regency looking glass is that designed to stand above a mantelshelf. Generally wider than it is high, its frame is painted white and the frieze is decorated with raised gilt ornaments, human figures in the flowing draperies of the Grecian style and perhaps a chariot. Sheraton had made cheval glasses popular, full-length looking glasses for bedrooms, swinging on reeded round or plain square pillars standing each on a pair of concave curving legs, and cheval glasses continued right through the 19th century.

The Regency produced a great variety of chairs. There were the extremely elegant ones copied from the designs on Ancient Greek vases with a deep top rail shaped to the human back and inlaid with brass or ebony stringing. The legs, usually completely plain, swept outwards in a curve like a sabre blade. Then there were those copied from the French Directoire style. Like all dictatorships, the Napoleonic one encouraged militarism, and furniture styles displayed martial emblems, sometimes rather incongruously like a miniature cannon with a clockface in its wheel. The English adopted these motifs, but they preferred to associate them with their own national heroes. After Nelson's death in 1805 chairs appeared with their backs carved to represent the drapes on his funeral catafalque. (Though the tradition that ebony stringing on many pieces of furniture was a mourning tribute to him does not stand up. Ebony stringing had been fashionable for several years before Trafalgar.) A rather more practical form of acknowledging England's naval greatness was the delightful cable chairs, so called because the spiral reeding of their back rails and legs resembles rope.

Another maritime, if not strictly naval, motif was the dolphin which crops up in odd places, usually as a support, for example as a bracket with its head forming the foot and a table top set on its tail.

The campaigns in Egypt early in the century led to an interest in that ancient civilisation and sphinxes were incorporated into many furniture designs, such as ornaments on the top corners of the bottom halves of secretaires and bureau-bookcases.

Regency designers took the development of the pillar table a stage further. They mounted circular or oval tops on massive central pedestals. These pedestals – sometimes referred to as 'monopodiums' – rise from a platform and are wider at the base than the top. Usually their four sides are concavely curved so that, although extremely robust, they do not look unduly cumbersome. The platform has short feet with good firm casters. For the longer, extending tables tripods were used, but of a different form from the previous cabriole legged type. The legs splayed outwards from the top and were longer than before, so that the turned post which supported the table top was shorter. The feet of these outward curving legs were almost horizontal so they required a different type of caster. It was in the form of an acanthus leaf neatly draped over the wheel. Towards the end of the period the acanthus leaf was superseded by a lion's paw; one can trace the descent of the theme from the old ball-and-claw.

Both pedestal and tripod supports were used for smaller tables like the circular 'drum-top' ones for use in libraries. The tops were covered with leather, often dyed red or green and with gold tooling, and the deep frieze contained drawers.

The Pembroke table, although pretty old-fashioned by now, continued to be made, doubtless because it was such a sensible item of furniture. Sofa tables had been made in the late 18th century but Regency ones are much more often found because of the greater popularity of sofas, daybeds, settees, couches and

113

*chaise-longues* which suited the elegant lolling of the period. A sofa table was like a Pembroke table, except that the flaps were at the ends, not the sides, and the rectangular centre portion was longer, and instead of a leg at each corner they had a pair at each end, joined by a stretcher. The legs themselves were let into a platform from which rose a solid panel, vase-shaped, or perhaps a single column. A charming revival was the use of a lyre and I must say I think it looks much better at the end of a sofa table than it does, as Adam used it, for the back of a chair.

A piece of furniture which, to me, typifies the Regency, is the drinking table. Composed of arcs of concentric circles, it has – or had, they haven't often survived – a bag hung on the shorter side to catch the empties. Often there was a brass screen to stop the bottles overshooting the bag and landing in the fire. The Regency bucks would gather round the longer curved side of the table and settle themselves down to arguing, discussion, wagering, and drinking bottle after bottle of claret port or brandy. Usually this sort of thing went on in the library or some such masculine room but I do know of one house where thick ropes of different colours lead from the dining room up the broad staircase each to a bedroom, so that host and guests could heave themselves, hand over hand, straight from the dining table to the bed. (Within living memory these ropes have been used for their original purpose.)

Regency sideboards needed to be – and were – substantial. They generally take the form of a rectangular table with a brass rail from which was hung the 'splashback' curtain, supported by inverted pyramidal pedestals containing cupboards one of which has shelves and the other leadlined to act as a wine-cooler.

The taste of this roisterous age is well illustrated by the furniture designed by George Smith who published *A Collection of Designs for Household Furniture and Interior Decoration* in 1808. (Long-winded titles were the fashion then, and at least they do tell the prospective buyer what to expect.) The designs are practical from a constructional point of view but the bewildering array of animals, both factual and mythological, lacks the erudition of Thomas Hope and, oddly enough, are much less way-out.

Vigorous, gaudy and superbly made, Regency furniture has little of the delicacy of detail of the work of thirty and forty years earlier. Marquetry was right out of fashion and the commode, that supreme expression of combined artistry and craftsmanship, had been replaced by the chiffonier, shelves set above a cupboard.

The rip-roaring times of the Regency could not last for ever and they gave place to an entirely different set of manners and moral outlook. Inevitably the change would be reflected in the furniture.

Much the same thing happened in America. The great Duncan Phyfe started by making furniture which combined the lightness of Sheraton's style with the solidity of the French Empire but by about 1825 even his furniture had degenerated into coarser heavier expression.

It is as if the furniture, both in Britain and America, followed the progress of the Regency bucks. Slim, supple and elegant in 1800, thirty years of over-eating and over-drinking made them heavy, paunchy, and not too particular about their appearance. So it was with the furniture.

# CHAPTER TWELVE

# *1830-1900 Victoriana.*
# *The Age of the Hypocrites*

IT is only within the last few years that we have begun to re-assess the furniture made during the long reign of Queen Victoria. Previously it was all lumped together as hideous and tasteless. Now, however, we are starting to pick out the plums from the heavy suet pudding and to appreciate them, not perhaps quite as their makers did, but at least without hostility.

There is no doubt that an awful lot of really ghastly stuff was produced during those sixty prosperous years, but many fine things were made, too. There were still brilliant designers, highly skilled craftsmen, and exacting patrons. But, on the other hand, there were new methods of construction which approached mass production, and a lack of discrimination coupled with a desire for ostentation. There was, in fact, a demand for second-rate furniture and an ample supply to meet it.

The Victorians regarded their homes as tremendously important. They were outward and visible signs of success and the wealth it had brought. Family life was the rock upon which all else was built, and the home was the effective expression of its stability. Comfort and solid worth were the aims, but unfortunately the Victorians didn't bother much about beauty. Size was more important. The catalogue of the Great Exhibition of 1851 devoted a great deal of space to emphasising the vast dimensions of furniture and other products, and it proudly and prominently proclaims the weights of various pieces of ponderous marble sculpture while paying scant attention to the aesthetic merits of the designs.

But while this Exhibition is generally agreed to represent the nadir of taste (or was until quite recently), one must not forget that the same Prince Consort who was its motivating source and presiding genious was also the man who drew attention to the long-ignored wonders of Italian Primitive painting.

This clash of sensibility and tastelessness is typical of the Victorian age as a whole, and is what makes it difficult to detect any consecutive theme. In reality, there wasn't any. There was just a flood of new ideas, some good, some bad, many horrible. Some died stillborn, others gained instant acceptance and underwent the usual pattern of imitation, improvement, distortion and decline.

An analogy has often been drawn between the furniture of the centuries and the seasons of the year. Spring in the 17th century, high summer in the 18th, autumn in the Regency followed by the Victorian winter. I agree with this, except on two points. Firstly, winter is usually followed by spring, and I haven't seen much sign of it so far. Secondly, I do think there was a brief Indian summer from about 1830 to 1845, covering the reign of dear old William IV, whose pine-apple head was not much bothered with matters of aesthetic taste, and the very early years of the young Queen Victoria. Before she ascended the throne on the death of 'Silly Billy' she lived at Kensington Palace and her bedroom there, now part of the London Museum, beautifully illustrates the taste of a year or two before her accession. It's a bit prim, but light and delicate, neither emphatic like the Regency nor sombre like the mid-19th century. But as princess she exerted no influence at all on fashion in decoration, and as Queen she only applauded Prince Albert's choice of everything, including the tartan carpets and covers at Balmoral.

But I must justify this Indian summer of which I speak. In a sentence, it was restrained Regency. The dolphins didn't flick their tails so vigorously, the joyousness went out of furniture, and it looked as if it had been left out in the sun and begun to melt. If the furniture of the late 18th century seems to have been drawn with a very sharp pencil that of the

1830s and '40s looks as though the pencil has become blunt. All the ingredients were still there, but the soufflé had gone a bit flat. However, as yet it was by no means a solid pudding, that was ten or fifteen years away.

The sweeping lines of chair legs which had been so graceful in Regency times were now replaced by straight turned ones which were ill-matched to the wide curved top rail extending beyond the uprights, which had survived from the earlier period. This was the beginning of the decline, but still only the beginning. The *papier mâché* chairs of the period achieved considerable elegance, but this was probably dictated more by the lightness of the material than by any conscious effort. When inlaid with shell and mother-of-pearl, as it nearly always was, it was very pretty. This prettiness effectively masks the faults in proportion of small caskets and cabinets and, to a great extent, of the chairs. But with their fragile legs and cane seats went disproportionately thick back frames so that they give the impression of a head too big for a body. This style, which is sometimes called 'balloon back' looks better in mahogany. The Victorians were great believers in chamfering edges and rounding corners, and 'balloon backs' had, instead of the rectangular top rail, a shaped curved one which merged with the uprights which were waisted and joined by a lateral splat. Many of them are well-proportioned and quite delightful.

Two changes in the general fashions of furnishing had appeared in the Regency and they were to gain ground throughout the early and mid-Victorian years. One was that the formality of 18th century arrangement of furniture gave place to a studied carelessness. Small pieces were dotted about the rooms, not ranged against the walls, and by the 1860s they were grossly overcrowded. It must have been a hazardous business to weave your way from one end of a drawing room to the other, dodging the whatnots, the chairs, the myriad occasional tables, particularly for women wearing the enormous crinolines which fashion dictated.

The other furnishing style which had its genesis in the Regency was that of softening austere lines by the use of drapery. But the Victorians were not content with long curtains and elaborate pelmets. They draped everything they could – tables, mantelshelves, any flat surface. The consequence was that there was little need to decorate something which would never be seen, hence the plainness of table tops.

However, it was a gradual process, and in the years leading up to the middle of the century there was a revival of interest in surface decoration. Marquetry was used with great effect on chiffoniers, small tables, and, in the grander houses, doors. Walnut veneers inlaid with lighter woods cast a warm and sunny glow in many a bedroom and drawing room. In fact inlay never entirely went out again, though after the middle of the century it was confined to that furniture which could not be covered with textiles, in other words fronts not tops. But it was carving that the Victorians really liked, and they couldn't have too much of it. The quality of the carving was often very fine but it differed from previous ideas in two fundamental ways. Firstly it was almost an end in itself. A sideboard or a cupboard was simply a convenient vehicle for the display of carving, rather than a piece of decorated furniture. Secondly, the Victorians favoured naturalistic representation, preferably of dead animals. A hare and a brace of partridges, exquisitely carved, or perhaps some pigeons and a few trout, were considered tasteful adornments for a massive sideboard in a country house. These still lifes – perhaps still deaths would be a better description – persisted throughout the 19th century and they form perhaps the one coherent link between the changes and fluctuations in the style and material of furniture.

By the time of the Great Exhibition in 1851 there was a bewildering confusion of styles. The Indian summer was over. England was in the process of changing over to an industrial society, and the furniture reflects the rapid and often uneasy transition. The position was additionally complicated by a conflict between two architectural styles, the Gothic and the classical and furniture made a convenient battlefield.

While the 'Gothick' of Walpole and Beckford had been a matter of dilettante whimsy, 19th century Gothic was, at least at first, a desperately serious matter. An earnest young architect, August Northmore Welby Pugin had carried out the interior decoration for Barry's Houses of Parliament and had convinced himself that the Gothic style was the only one worth bothering about. (Perhaps he had not noticed that the Houses of Parliament are fundamentally classical in proportion though entirely Gothic in detail.) Pugin was a religious fanatic and he reasoned that medieval churches and cathedrals had been built to the glory of God and were therefore good. Classical architecture was based on pagan temples and was therefore bad. Whether it is reasonable to equate architecture with morals is debatable, but anyway Pugin did.

All his work – his furniture designs as well as his ecclesiastical and domestic architecture – has complete integrity. He never skimped or took short cuts. And he took the trouble to discover precisely what the people he was trying to emulate had done, and how they did it.

Unfortunately the imitators of Pugin himself did not. Interest in the medieval styles increased mightily as the 19th century advanced but both architecture and furniture grew less and less like the products of the Middle Ages.

Not, of course, that the classical styles fared much better in the hands of the Victorians. Those tall gaunt London houses with their clumsy and coarse plasterwork were the saddest examples that the whole long classical movement produced. But the two conflicting styles, diametrically opposed in ideology as well as in execution, dominated the 19th century. Small wonder, then, that the furniture styles echoed the architectural confusion.

Fortunately for us, when we try to make some sense out of all this incoherence, the Victorian age was punctuated by a series of exhibitions, and an examination of their catalogues shows, if not changes in the fashions of furniture, at least switches in the trends. The 1862 exhibition contained furniture which was very different from that of eleven years earlier. It was vaguely Italian Renaissance in character, and the walnut and mahogany were used in the solid rather than as veneers. The curves were more restrained and the overall appearance was less bloated. Carving there was, of course, but it didn't sprawl all over everything. It was contained in panels, with the blessed relief of plain space in between. The carving itself was deeply cut, and skilfully executed. The human form now joined the animal, usually in the form of caryatids like figure-heads on ships' prows.

In the mid-'50s interior decoration crossed a new threshold of pain with the invention of aniline dyes. Hitherto the soft hues of vegetable dyes had prevented the clashing of colours but the strident electric blues, mustard yellows, and shrieking greens were uncompromising. Ten years later they had become universal, and the drawing-rooms of the mid-'60s, so many of which have been preserved in photographs (mercifully monochrome) show patterns everywhere, all reflected in huge sheets of looking glass in gilt frames.

It was into this welter of bad taste that William Morris plunged. He was appalled by the debasement of design and particularly by the shoddy work of machine-made furniture. But instead of having a go at the manufacturers he tried, Canute-like, to stem the tide by a return to the cottage crafts of the Middle Ages. He himself did not actually design furniture but his associates did, and they thought along the same lines. One of them, Philip Webb the architect, designed some very plain tables in unstained oak, with massive wooden nails. They were in complete contrast to the prevailing taste, and it was not until right at the end of the century that they – or rather designs inspired by them – came into fashion. Another of Morris's associates, Ford Madox Brown, designed cheap bedroom furniture for servants, and this was much copied though seldom with the clean plain lines of the originals. Another of the firm's successful design was the 'Morris chair' with an adjustable back.

A style which had far more immediate impact than Morris's was that shown in *Gothic Forms, applied to Furniture, Metalwork, etc. for Interior Purposes* by Bruce Talbert which was published in 1867 and by Charles Eastlake's *Hints on Household Taste* published a year later.

The iron bedsteads with half-testers can hardly be called beautiful but at least they were a refreshing change from the heavy, claustrophobic fourposters of the time. Sideboards, too, were the exact opposite of those animal-encrusted monsters of ten years before. Solid and stolid, they were uncompromisingly four-square and entirely shorn of carving. In America, Talbert's contribution to this new style was ignored and it became known – and still is – as the 'Eastlake style'.

In essence, it was clean-lined style, but it very soon became debased, and the clean lines became blurred. The sideboards of only ten years later were less like utilitarian kitchen dressers, and they sprouted shelves in unlikely places, and where Talbert and Eastlake had inserted painted panels their imitators began to place looking glass. The style soon became gimcrack and it had, anyway, to meet the competition of the manufacturers who were producing in huge quantities ghastly travesties of Elizabethan furniture in oak, stained black to convey the impression of age. But, nasty though I find them, I think I prefer them to the spindly, fussy things into which the Eastlake style finally degenerated.

The large-scale manufacturers were, of course, quite unmoved by any of the *avant-garde* ideas. Manufacturing was already big business but it was still really in its infancy. Labour conditions – and labour relations – were right in the middle of the 'dark Satanic mills' era and all that the owners were concerned with was supplying the demand and if the demand was for shiny black crude oak they did not argue. They just supplied it. The letters, autobiographies, and diaries of the 19th century, fascinating though many of them are, seldom mention furnishing, whereas their 18th century equivalents are full of it. If there did not exist the evidence of the taste of Victorian times one would be able to deduce its paucity from this lack of interest in it. The apathy and ignorance was widespread but, naturally, there were exceptions. Items specially made for exhibitions displayed the finest craftsmanship and even though the designs may have lacked the genius of the 18th century the skills were as great as ever.

In the 1870s and '80s even the Victorian palates had become jaded with the eternal rehashing of 16th and 17th century menus. They welcomed with eagerness anything new, and the opening up of trade with Japan provided a happy distraction. After the Paris exhibition of 1862 and the London one of 1867 at both of which Japanese designs were shown, a great deal of rather horrid furniture appeared in England, claiming inspiration from the land of the Chrysanthemum Throne. But mostly it was spindly imitation bamboo, usually painted pale yellow, and much of it mercifully disintegrated years ago. There was also, in the 1880s, a short vogue for imitation of Indian, Egyptian, Turkish and other exotic designs. But with England at the height of her commercial power, it was easy enough to import the genuine articles and the interest in the substitutes soon wihered and died. It was considered better to buy a Benares gong which had been made in Birmingham and sent out to India than one which came from Birmingham direct.

In direct opposition to this trend was the conservative taste for the heavy, the solid, and the dull. Shiny mahogany, artificially coloured dark red, was far more usual for dining tables than natural oak, and colours of draperies and wallpapers had toned down very considerably from the first brash exploitation of aniline dyes. The bobble-fringed covers which still adorned, if that's the right word, mantelshelves and tables were usually bottle-green or muddy brown, except that in dining rooms deep crimson was held to aid digestion.

But by 1880 or a few years after, there were stirrings of revolt. Handicraft societies started to be formed and soon the 'Arts and Crafts Movement' became a flood. The various societies, separately or jointly, organised exhibitions, published magazines and catalogues, and generally succeeded in making people think about furnishing and furniture. The movement had many aspects, often contradictory. There was fairly plain 'honest' oak, light in colour. There was a good deal of light-weight but dark-painted stuff, there were sideboards incorporating stained glass, chairbacks cut out in heart shapes or padded with velvet hearts secured with large brass-headed nails.

The plainer furniture settled down into a style which became not unlike the Scandinavian furniture of fifty years later, and the more finicky stuff blossomed out, right at the end of the century into *Art Nouveau*.

But not everybody, not even most people, cared for these *avant-garde* ideas. They wanted something new, but not as new as all that. So one important facet of the Arts and Crafts Movement was a revival of interest in the styles of eight or a hundred years before. They looked up the old pattern books and made furniture to the designs they found in them. Sheraton seems to have been the most popular and indeed this movement is sometimes called the 'Sheraton Revival'. But older styles were copied, and Chippendale and Hepplewhite were not forgotten. Walnut, satinwood and mahogany were used just as they had been and, except for the varnishing and the metalwork, these pieces might have been made in the 18th, not the 19th century. However, they were made by craftsmen who took pride in their work and who often liked to introduce little ideas of their own, so that the copies are seldom exact. Extremely well made, they are pleasant pieces of furniture and they are sufficiently different from the 18th century work to escape the stigma of being fakes. It was a style in its own right, even if a rather mediocre one.

It followed that if the designs of the 18th century were worth copying then perhaps the furniture itself wasn't so bad after all. The Late Victorians dragged it out of its hiding places and looked at it with a new eye. Just as we have been doing ever since.

# CHAPTER THIRTEEN

# Genuine or Junk?

THE more one knows about antique furniture the less likely one is to mistake a fake for the genuine article. That much is entirely obvious. What is just as important, and much more difficult, is to avoid mistaking the genuine article for the fake. But before I go into the latter proposition, let us be quite clear what we mean by genuine and fake.

A genuine piece is one which was made at the time and in the style from which it appears to date, and has remained unaltered ever since. A fake is one which has been made in the right style but the wrong time. In other words, when the maker has deliberately set out to deceive.

But between black and white there are many shades of grey. A genuine piece may have been heavily restored, it may have been embellished, it may have been altered or it may have started life as two separate pieces of furniture which have later been 'married'. A fake may be a reproduction, in which case there was no intention to deceive although the result may be the same.

To take them in order, the restored piece can usually be detected if it is examined closely. The new wood is likely to be of a slightly different colour from the old and the join can be felt by the fingertips even if it is not obvious to the eye. The important thing is to know where to look and this is a matter of commonsense. All one has to do is to imagine which parts of the pieces have been most likely show signs of wear, and which parts are least likely to have stood up to such wear. I would, for instance, be suspicious of an Elizabethan oak chest on which

E                                                                    125 the feet showed no sign of having been banged by mops and brooms over the years. For chairs a very good test is to move them, sit in them, and get up again, noting where your hands naturally fall. It is a safe bet that if you grasp the top of the back rail to move the chair, or rest your hands on the ends of the arms to heave yourself out of it, other people will have touched it in the same places for the same purposes. Over the years this will show. If it doesn't, that particular part has been replaced. If there is no sign of wear on any of these places the whole thing is probably a fake.

It is inconceivable that a chest-of-drawers or a tallboy can have had a couple of hundred years use without showing some signs of it. Bits will have been chipped out of the veneer and stuck on again, or replaced by another section which cannot be an exact match. This is perfectly acceptable, providing the repair has been well done and there is not an undue amount of damage. If the piece is in pristine condition have a look at the drawers which are easiest to reach. They are the ones which will have been used most, and their runners, and the parts of the carcase, on which they rest, will show whether the drawer has been pulled out and pushed in as much as one would expect.

Do not expect an antique to be perfect – that is literally too good to be true. People kick the ends of table legs, they push salt cellars across polished surfaces (your true lover of antiques lifts the salt cellar up and puts it down again, he never slides it). So a certain amount of fair wear and tear must be accepted, and be very cautious if it isn't there. A massive repair is quite another thing. It may not make the piece unacceptable but it will certainly reduce its value. Here again, detection is largely a matter of commonsense. Visualise the use to which the piece has been put and determine what parts of it have had to bear the greatest burdens. Then look at them and see if they betray any signs of having been renewed. Typical instances might be a fragile chairback in which the shield or splat has been replaced, or an early tallboy whose stand has given way. Chairs have had a new leg or two, canework has been renewed, the end posts of a fourposter bed of the 16th century are of later date than the headboard. (I have never quite been able to understand how even the most energetic housemaid could break one of these sturdy posts with the flick of a duster, but I have seen so many new posts on old beds that I have come to the conclusion that these sturdy hunks of wood must be more delicate than they look.)

The embellished piece is a sad affair, mutton dressed as lamb. These things started life as plain, honest, possibly country-made pieces, and years later some chiseller inflicted horrible wounds on them. The trouble was that when the late Victorians and Edwardians swung away from the furniture of their own time and began to appreciate antiques they did not entirely abandon – and how could they be expected to – the taste of their own time. And that taste was for carving and intricate decoration. The consequence was that the dealers pandered to them, and served up ornate carving. If a piece had been made without carving that was easily remedied. Easily, that is, to a standard which would deceive somebody who had no clear idea of what furniture of that period ought to look like. But the great difference, which cannot be disguised, is between carving which was originally cut out of a piece of wood and stood proud from it, and carving which has been done later and necessarily incised into it. This is a very good guide, but unfortunately it is not infallible. Some – though by no means all – carving throughout the 17th century was incised, usually in the form of grooves to decorate a spandrel. Therefore one does occasionally find perfectly genuine 17th century oak pieces with this incised work. However, I do not ever remember seeing a piece of mahogany with original incised carving.

However, I vividly remember seeing a noble mahogany and satinwood bureau of the late 18th century with horrible scars on its sides where somebody had cut *Art Nouveau* tulips into the poor thing's flanks.

Those delightful round-topped tables of the mid 18th century fell an easy prey to the vandals. The pie-crust versions (see chapter ten) were considered to be best, by early collectors, so pie-crust they had to be. Now, the original pie-crusts were gouged out of a very thick plank of mahogany, the plain tops from a rather thinner one. Not all that thin, and just thick enough for

127

a skilful faker to plane away enough to leave a raised edge. Happily, though, the old screws went firmly into two-thirds of the depth of the timber and when the top was shaved away they stuck out like sore thumbs. A simple matter to file off the ends of the screws, but utterly impossible to conceal the holes, however carefully they were plugged. So, when you see a pie-crust table with a thin top look carefully along the top to find the plugs. You will.

A much less heinous form of embellishment is the fitting of new handles, as long as they do not alter the whole character of the piece. Wooden handles began to appear on furniture in the late Regency and they continued throughout Victorian times. There is a theory that, during the Napoleonic wars, brass was required for munitions and that metal furniture handles were melted down to provide it, in the way that many London squares lost their elegant railings during the 1939-1945 war. Be that as it may there is no doubt that the Victorians had a great incentive to get rid of old-fashioned metal handles and to replace them with the latest wooden knobs. It made the piece of furniture look more up-to-date, and brought it into line with the fashion of the time. Also the tinkers who went round mending brass and copper cooking pots would have been glad to give a few pennies for brass which they could so easily melt down and use to patch a saucepan.

When people began collecting antiques they admired the 18th century but thought nothing of the Regency, which did not really become popular until after the Second World War. Always ready to oblige, the dealers of the early days of collecting whipped the genuine wooden knobs off Regency furniture and replaced them with copies of the metal handles of the late 18th century. They then served up the result as 'Sheraton', and everybody was happy.

What with all these goings-on it is fairly uncommon to find a piece of furniture with its original metal handles, and when it has the dealer is quick to point them out. Happily, it is easy to tell whether the handles are genuine or not; not by looking at them, but by looking inside the drawer or door. Wooden knobs have quite thick shafts and when they are removed they leave a large round hole. On the front of the drawer this can be disguised by covering it with a metal backplate, but inside the plug is there for all to see, as long, of course, as they take the trouble to open the drawer and look.

Hinges, too, have seldom lasted the course. The new ones are usually of a different shape from the old, so the outline of the old hinge will be seen on the inside of the door or lid. The new hinge will have machine-made screws, probably of steel rather than brass, and of a uniform shape. The screwheads will be a perfect circle, which hand-made ones never were. To rate as an absolutely genuine piece, the hinges must be original. But one can carry purism beyond the bounds of common sense, and I would never refrain from buying an otherwise genuine piece of furniture just because it had new hinges, though I would probably haggle over the price. But then I always do.

Sometimes a restoration can amount to an alteration, which will change the apparent date. If it makes the piece look earlier than it is, the alteration was probably done with this in mind, and done within the present century. For instance I have recently seen a country-made food cupboard which probably dates from the early 19th century. It is crudely constructed but although it is of oak which was cheap and unfashionable it has the proportions of the late 18th century. It originally had wooden knob handles and it is this feature, together with the ham-handed way the thing was made, which causes me to put a rather later date on it than I otherwise would. But when the wooden knobs were taken off they were replaced by pear drop handles of a pattern which dates from the second half of the 17th century. It is likely that this alteration was made during the last seventy years with the express purpose of passing the piece off as 17th century.

Alterations which suggest a different date work the other way too. Supposing this food cupboard had really been of the second half of the 17th century it would originally have had bun feet. If it had stood on a stone-flagged floor for a hundred years the feet might have rotted away with the constant washing of the floor. If the owner at the time had cause to renew the feet he would probably have had the new ones made as brackets, in the latest fashion. He would have valued the food cupboard as a food cupboard, not because it was old.

So although there is the golden rule that you date a piece of furniture by its latest feature, you have to be sure that the latest feature is part of the original structure.

An entirely different type of alteration is the one which has been made with the deliberate intention of enhancing the value. We do not possess the amount of space in our homes which our ancestors enjoyed, and consequently we seldom have room for large pieces of furniture. It is, therefore, the smaller pieces which fetch the highest prices. It is usually possible to reduce the size of a piece and this has often been done both for convenience and to make it more valuable. This is seldom done to tables because it would make them look ridiculous, like a man wearing a hat several sizes too small. But any furniture with drawers is an open invitation to the faker. However, he seldom goes to the trouble of making new dovetails on the side of the drawer he has shortened so all one need do is to compare the drawer sides. In the unlikely event of him having repeated the old dovetail he still has the problem of the handles which will be off centre. He must, therefore, move them, and herein lies his downfall. He can botch up the front of the drayer with new backplates but the interior of the drawer front will betray him. Bureaux and bureau-bookcases are particularly suspect. Even the best 18th century craftsmen didn't bother to polish or veneer the top of the bureau which would be hidden by the bookcase, so always look closely to see whether the top of a bureau has been veneered at a later date. If it has it will look different from the sides.

The bookcase part will look pretty peculiar, all on its own sitting on the floor. And as 18th century bookcases didn't sit on the floor – except the big ones and they almost always had cupboards under the shelves – I would steer clear of anything which looked as unhappy as that. In fact once you have become accustomed to the look of antique furniture you will be able to tell the altered piece ten yards off, by the wrong proportions alone.

This principle applies equally to what are called 'married

pieces'. I must confess that I have done this myself. I had a nice little tripod table – a country-made thing of oak – but the top had been broken in a removal. Rather than throw the whole table away, I searched round and found one with a leg broken off the tripod. So I 'married' the two and I am quite happy with the result, and not in the least ashamed of it. But I wouldn't be nearly so keen if I were offered a bureau-bookcase which had started out as a bureau and had a fake bookcase stuck on top of it to increase the price. I would ask the dealer to lift the top off, and if the bureau part had a carefully veneered top I would ask searching questions.

Next, the reproduction. You see them, new, in furniture shops everywhere. There is not the slightest intention to deceive, and indeed only the very naïve could be deceived. They very, very seldom reproduce the originals exactly. 'Suggested by the designs of Chippendale' – or Hepplewhite or Sheraton or whatever – is as far as they could possibly go. They are mass-produced by modern methods and you can tell them a mile off. Unfortunately it isn't quite as easy as that. The 'Sheraton Revival' at the end of the 19th century produced some pieces which really did look like the products of a hundred years before, and seventy years of use has given them an appearance of age. However, you can fall back on the difference in the screws, and, in the case of furniture with doors, the reddened interiors will give them away. The makers did not, of course, attempt to deceive their customers and they openly used the methods of their own day and not previous ones.

A very important clue is given by the surface. All Sheraton Revival furniture was French polished. Up until about 1820 when French polish came into use, new furniture was treated with a varnish comprised of spirits and a vegetable oil. It did not give a very high gloss and the patina on old furniture is the result of centuries of polishing with beeswax and turpentine. In the later years of the Regency period this laborious but effective – oh so effective – treatment was replaced by the system coming from France. French polishing gave – and gives – a high gloss and a glass-like finish. It looks shiny but there is no depths to it. In the 19th and early 20th centuries much honest old furniture fell victim to the French polisher. The lovely deep patina bestowed by centuriees of loving care was swept away and the result bears about as much relationship to the original as convenience foods do to roast beef and Yorkshire pudding.

Today the high gloss is achieved by spraying the innocent wood in the way that a car is sprayed.

An antique which has escaped the French polisher is more highly priced – and rightly so – than one which hasn't.

Unfortunately the history of reproductions doesn't end – or rather begin – there. One does, from time to time, find articles in a style of an age earlier than that in which they were made, even though they were in fact made long before people valued antiques. Why this should have happened I don't quite know. Possibly somebody already had one piece and wanted another matching it. For instance, the table illustrated at Plate 31 looks at first sight to have been made at the end of the 17th century, except that it has 19th century wooden knobs. But they could well have been fitted afterwards. As a matter of fact, the provenance of this table is unusually reliable. The man who had it made told the story to his grand-daughter whose daughter told it to me. The story is this. One day, in about 1830, he was walking up his drive when a large branch fell off an oak tree, missing his head by inches. It is extremely unusual for an oak – unlike an elm – suddenly to shed a branch on a clear still day, and in order to commemorate the event this character instructed his estate carpenter to make him a table out of it.

Horribly often the stories handed down in families are wildly distorted or have no basis in fact at all. But in this case I am inclined to believe it. The table is competently made but a fine craftsman of 1830 – or 1840, allowing time for the wood to season – would have done a better job. The wooden knobs are without doubt original, so the date is authentic. One can only presume that the man who ordered it already had a late 17th century table and told his man to copy it.

Whatever it is, it certainly isn't a fake. A fake is made with the intention to deceive. Old wood is used, from a larger piece of furniture or one that has been damaged beyond repair. The fakers were – and still are, though happily there are less of them about nowadays – both knowledgeable and skilful. They were up to all the tricks, and they bashed the things about to give the signs of wear. I wish I could give some sovereign remedy to protect you against fakes but I can't. The best advice I can give is to look underneath and see whether the places where the hand rests when the piece is moved show a smooth and dark patch. Fakers did not usually bother about that sort of thing.

But take heart. Labour is so expensive today that it is seldom worth faking any but the most expensive piece. This isn't very encouraging because it means that the more you pay the more likely you are to be buying a fake, but it does mean that any middle-priced article is likely to be genuine. The best plan is to be absolutely certain in your own mind that the thing is genuine before you buy it. If you have any doubt, don't. No man is so unloved that he lacks kind friends ever ready to point out his mistakes.

In this way you will undoubtedly miss buying many a genuine piece, but that is the price of caution. And remember that dealers are, on the whole, honest men. They are handling antiques all day and every day, and they develop a sixth sense. They are human and not infallible, but they aren't very often wrong. So don't be too proud to listen to a dealer's advice. He probably hopes that you will be a satisfied customer and come back for more.

Once you have acquired your antique you will want to look after it properly. When I buy a new piece – or rather an old piece new to me – I first of all wash it, but not with anything as drastic as soap and water. For oak I use beer, but for other woods I use a mixture of half water and half vinegar. I rub the thing all over with a duster dipped in a saucer of this mixture. Then I take a dry duster and go over it again, rubbing very lightly. This is to smear the mixture well, and not leave any globules which will dry white. Then I go away for several hours, at least four.

When I return my heart sinks. The piece is lack-lustre and coated with a dull powder, almost slime. In wild panic I seize a clean dry duster and rub it tentatively over the surface. If it glides along and leaves a shining trail, all is well. If the surface is still tacky I leave it a bit longer. In the end the dirt of ages comes off on the duster, and leaves the piece of furniture bright, but begging for food. This I give it, by using a proprietary polish, though not one which contains silicones because they make it look glassy, like French polish. I leave the polish to soak in for ten minutes or so and then I rub all the polish off. That is all.

New marks – except burns – usually come off with the water and vinegar treatment, but old ones need a stronger treatment. The best method I know – and even that doesn't always work – is to mix a little olive oil into a paste with salt. (The salt is only a vehicle to make the oil easier to handle and to place.) Then I apply it, rubbing gently with my finger tips. After a few hours I gently lift the paste off the stain, a sheet of writing paper is ideal for this. If the mark has not gone I try again two days later, by which time the oil has had a chance to dry out. But do be careful not to overdo it, otherwise the oil itself will leave a dark stain.

I quite realise that all this entails a lot of work. But worth it, don't you think?

CHAPTER FOURTEEN
# *Starting a Collection*

IF you want to buy an antique go into a church. This is not as mad as it sounds. You will not find the antique you want to buy and they wouldn't sell it to you if you did. But visiting churches is the best way I know of finding out about the general trends and fashions in antiques.

The reason is that almost all churches, except the very modern ones, have memorials and monuments which date from past centuries. And these stone or marble plaques are invariably similiar in style – though not of course in shape – to the furniture contemporary with them. If you examine the decoration on the monuments you will find that it is remarkably similar to that on furniture of the same time. And not only is it the same kind of decoration, but it is also on the same scale. That is to say that the motifs on a frieze are in exactly the same proportion to one another as they are on, for instance, the frieze of a table. They may all be bigger or smaller, but their size in relationship to one another will be uniform, and they will be spaced at the same intervals as they would be on furniture.

But why, you may ask, should I look at stone and marble when what I am really interested in is wood? The answer is that church monuments always have one feature which is extremely rare on furniture – and that is a date.

Not one of them omits the date of the death of the man or woman whom it commemorates. One is, I think, safe in assuming that this date is correct. 'In lapidary inscriptions,' wrote Doctor Johnson, 'a man is not upon oath.' I am, sure, though, that when he wrote this he had in mind the qualities which were extolled on the monuments of his own 18th century. We are at liberty to take with a pinch of salt such eulogies as 'of amiable disposition and of ample fortune, she bore her many sufferings with a truly Christian. . . .' But when it comes to the date we are entitled to rely on its accuracy.

The mourning husband, wife, son, or whoever it might be, would hardly be likely to get the date wrong, or anyway not a year out. And he or she would naturally want the memorial to be as good as possible. Therefore the sculptor or mason employed must have been urged to do the best he could. It is highly unlikely that he would have deliberately adopted an archaic style, so we can take it that he was as up-to-date as he knew how to be.

Throughout this book I have emphasised the impossibility of clapping a precise date on any piece of furniture by its style alone. The maker, or the customer for whom it was made, may have been set in his ways and had a marked preference for the styles which had been in vogue when he was young. Or he may have been completely ignorant of what was happening outside his own little circle. But this all applies with rather less force to monuments in churches. The clergy have always been educated and well read, and sculptors and stonemasons have always had wide experience. (Unless the bereaved happened to choose one who had never done a memorial before and in that case he would almost certainly have been young and the young have always been in the latest fashion, the latest vogue, with it, or whatever the current description of modernity happend to be.) On the whole, I think we can safely assume that monuments and memorials were executed in the most up-to-date style. Allow a year for getting the whole thing organised and executed and you have an accurately dated example of the prevailing style.

It's rather fun to try to guess the date while you are too far away to read it. In a surprisingly short time you will find that you recognise the difference in styles at a glance and that your guesses are seldom more than five or ten years out. You will begin to pick out the features which can be related to furniture, the strapwork, the egg-and-dart mouldings, the swan-necked pediments, the urns. Even the lace on the handkerchief which wipes away the tear from the cheek of a mourning cherub will suggest the delicacy of carving which can be found on woodwork of the same period.

Having assimilated the general feel of the differing trends, the next step is to make a rather less oblique approach to the furniture itself. In the last ten years or so there has been a quiet revolution in museums. Today the exhibits are well lighted, well displayed, and very full information is available about every piece. Many museums show furniture in appropriate settings so that you can see the pieces in the sort of rooms for which they were made. You can relate panelling, plasterwork, fireplace and curtains to the furniture of the period.

Curators of museums are great experts and most of them are only too pleased to share their knowledge. But they are remarkably busy men and women so don't waste their time. Only go to them with your problem as a last resort, if you can't find the answer in any other way. Also remember that the displays in museums are seldom typical of any particular period. I do not mean that they are not accurate representations, of course they are, but unless they deliberately set out to show something different, the sets will be designed to display the best available furniture. Sadly, the best is never typical.

Museums, then, are rather like shop windows where only the most attractive goods are on show. The highest praise you can give a piece of furniture is to say that it is worthy of a place in a museum.

Another important and painless way of absorbing knowledge is to visit the great houses which are open to the public – Hampton Court, Chatsworth, Woburn Abbey and many more. Some were built and furnished in one glorious fell swoop. Others were enlarged and altered over the years, often over the centuries. Sometimes, again, furniture has been replaced by later styles as it wore out. But in all cases these houses are living history and, furthermore, especially if they have been in the same family for many generations the provenance of any particular piece of furniture is often well known. I remember sitting in the library of a great house and asking the owner about a fireplace I had noticed in some other room.

'Ah yes,' he said, 'that's made out of the marble which the third earl brought back from Siena when he went on the Grand Tour in 1728.' He then opened a drawer in a desk and took out the bill for carving this marble. The bill had lain in that drawer for more than two hundred years. (But do not be too envious of the owners of stately homes. One of them recently remarked to me, 'All I am is caretaker for three hundred years of other people's shopping.')

But, as with museums, great houses are typical only of the best furniture available at any one time. Their owners had to be rich to build or furnish them and there wouldn't have been much point in pouring out money on the building and then economising on the furniture.

But the fine furniture which you see in museums and stately homes differs only in degree from the majority of furniture produced at the same time. The proportions are the same, the woods are the same, the general style is the same. It is only the elaboration and the quality of the craftsmanship which makes the superb stand out from the very good.

This – visiting churches, museums and stately homes – is leading up to the next stage, which is spending hours and hours in auction rooms. But even now you are not ready to buy. The day will come when you can confidently walk into an auction room, but it has not come yet.

In the auction rooms you will see furniture in a fairly undressed state. It is the auctioneer's job to sell what has been brought him, not to prepare it for sale. If it has a chip out of the veneer or a handle broken or missing the auctioneer will not attempt to repair it. When the piece comes up for sale the buyer – private customer and dealer alike – will bear in mind the cost of the necessary repairs when he makes his bid and you yourself will soon learn to do so. But long before you reach the stage of bidding you will have learned a very great deal. In an auction room you can inspect the furniture closely and at your leisure. The particulars in the catalogue will be brief, but they will be correct as far as they go, except in very exceptional circumstances. The description of the more important pieces will be printed in capital letters, and any unusual feature – or indeed any feature which the auctioneer hopes will increase the value – will be commented on.

When you have seen half a dozen apparently similar pieces sold you will discover, from the prices they fetch, that one is considered more desirable than another, and if you have inspected both of them closely before the sale you will know why.

I have always found saleroom porters both knowledgeable and helpful. Handling furniture all day and every day, they have developed an instinct about it and they always seem ready to express an opinion. But they are there to do a job, and if you take up too much of their time their employers will not like it. So, like the museum curator, the saleroom porter should be treated with consideration and you must avoid wasting his time. (Museum curators do not expect to be tipped. Saleroom porters do.)

When you are thoroughly familiar with the furniture of all periods, as it passes through the salerooms, then – and only then – the time is ripe for you to start collecting.

But even then I would not advise you to bid at auction, unless you are perfectly confident. The dealers – and there are always dealers – have been buying at auctions for years and they know all about it. If they hang back and let you pick up what you think is a fantastic bargain it will probably turn out to be no more than an expensive lesson. It is far better to pay a little more for something which you can be sure about. In other words, get the expert dealer on your side. And this you do by going into his shop, not by outbidding him at an auction sale.

An antique dealer accepts, as part of his business, that customers like to talk about antiques. But he is human, and it is not reasonable to expect him to be interested in hearing about the piece of furniture you bought from someone else last year. What he is most interested in is what you are going to buy now. If you never buy anything, but you still continue to drop in for a cosy chat, he will soon discover pressing engagements elsewhere. So do not overdo it.

However, if once in a while you do buy something, he will be patient on the days when you are quite clearly not going to. It's all part of his after-sales service.

I don't think I have ever been into an antique shop, an auction room, or a museum without learning something. Nobody knows everything about antiques – or anything else, for that matter – and it is always fascinating to hear a couple of dealers discussing some particular piece. They are not airing their knowledge, they are trying to find out something they don't know already, each one hopes to hear something new and to give the other something new in return.

So try to find a friendly dealer and learn from him. You probably will not be able to tell him much that he doesn't know already, but a suitable reward in exchange for the information he gives you is to buy something from him.

But even the friendliest, most experienced dealer is not utterly infallible. So the final decision whether or not to acquire a particular piece of furniture must be yours, and yours alone. Try and imagine that you have come across the things in the middle of a field, with nothing and nobody to influence your decision. Judge it solely on what you consider to be its merits. You may be wrong but at least you will be satisfied that you have done your best.

26.
The rich glow of satinwood against the dark mahogany leads the eye upward
to the full glory of the exquisitely carved and shaped urns outlined on this bureau-
bookcase of 1770-1775. Compare with Plate 10. (Hotspur).

27.
The fine grain of the mahogany and the subtle shape are all that is needed for this late 18th century sideboard to achieve its effect. (Hotspur).

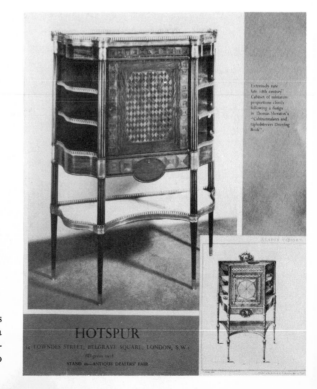

28.
The spindly legs of Thomas Sheraton's design for a 'ladys cabinet' greatly improved by translation into wood. (Hotspur).

29.
Mendlesham chairs were sophisticated versions of the Windsor principle in which the legs and back are separately mortised into the seat. This example, in private ownership, dates from approximately 1810.

30.
A typical rosewood Pembroke table of the Regency period shown with the flaps raised. (Hotspur).

31.

This small oak table might, at first glance, be thought to date from the late 17th century. (Compare with Plate 6). In fact it was made about 1830 for the great-great-grandfather of its present owner. See Chapter Thirteen.

32.

One of a pair of footstools made about 1870-1880. Originally the top was covered with wool in a pattern of red and green diamonds reinforced with steel beads. The use of cabuchon decorations and the scrolls above the stump feet are reminscent of the mid-18th century. Compare with Plate 23.

CHAPTER FIFTEEN
## *Odds and Ends of Antiques*

COLLECTING anything is an absorbing hobby, though nearly always demanding of both time and money. There is, of course, a strict limit to the time and money which the average person can afford to spend on antiques. However, one can have a great deal of fun picking up odd trifles of little worth and of small size. Particularly those things which do not fit into any precise category, neither furniture nor china, neither silver nor glass.

These oddments may not form the basis of a collection, but individually they can be ornamental or even useful. Seldom paying more than a pound, I have, over the years, acquired quite an assortment of unrelated items which have appealed to me for one reason or another. Many of them I have been able to find a use for, such as the battered old Persian bronze bowl still with traces of its silver coating which now does duty as an ashtray. Others have proved useless, such as the box I fell in love with when I saw it on a stall in a market. Originally it must have been a proud and splendid thing, but the passing centuries have dealt harshly with it. It is quite small, only about nine inches long and five deep and high. Its top is domed and is raised by a central handle, a loop of twisted silver wire. The box is veneered in red tortoiseshell, and the corners were once protected by silver gesso. A little brass lock, fashioned as delicately as a watch, once defended the box's contents against prying eyes and thieving fingers.

The tortoiseshell is chipped and scratched, all that remains of the silvered corners are lumps of dirty plaster with, here and there, a speck of silver, paper thin. Of the four dainty little bun feet only one sad lead ball remains, so that the box is pathetic in its lopsidedness.

For a few pence it became mine, and I carried it home tenderly, with compassion. It might, I thought, trying desperately to justify its purchase, come in useful for containing something – anything. But when I opened it – its key had disappeared long since – I found that the bottom of the box still retained, completely intact, its original lining of painted paper – a crudely done Biblical scene. The little box had, I felt, suffered enough. I could not bring myself to put in it anything which might scuff or tear the paper. So now it sits, unused and unusable, too damaged to be beautiful any more, a stupid bit of junk. But although it has lost almost everything one thing remains. The little box still has magic, at least for me. When I look at it I can go into a reverie and picture in my mind the honest craftsman who fashioned it nearly four hundred years ago. And I can imagine its first owner, an elegant lady of fashion at the Court of William and Mary why not, who kept the tortoiseshell combs for her piled-high hair in it, and without doubt her love letters. How sentimental can you get? All right, but if the things they knew and used and loved cannot speak to us of the generations long gone what can? If the answer is nothing you have no business to bother with antiques.

Another unconsidered trifle which set me off on a trip of nostalgia was a Victorian watch-stand. A scallop shell rested on scrolled wire legs and above it was a hooped back with a small hook welded to the top. It took no great feat of imagination to picture the first owner of that one. With a final twirl of his waxed moustache, and a smoothing of his hair, lustrous with macassar oil, he would prepare for bed. First the close-fitting long frockcoat would be carefully hung in the shiny red massive wardrobe. A few steps across the Turkey carpet and he would be beside the gleaming oxblood table on which stood this pretty little watch-stand. On the waiting hook he would carefully hang his gold watch, possible listening for a final count of its repeating chime. Then he would loop and curl the Albert chain until it nestled securely in the scallop shell.

To me the charm of this little watch-stand lies in its femininity.

It is so completely different from the essentially masculine pater-familias. So very much more akin to the submissive wife, coyly expectant between the glossy linen sheets of the great brass bed-stead.

But surely, I thought, such a pretty little object should never have been painted white. It cannot have been intended to look so clinical and austere. Very gingerly I applied a little paint-remover to the underside of the shell. Soon I was rewarded by a glimmer of gold and, pressing resolutely on, I peeled off the inept white paint until the ormulu shimmered dully. With a very weak solution of ammonia (a teaspoonful in quite a big bowl) I brought back the pale golden sheen and the little watch-stand stood revealed in all its pristine prettiness. Suddenly a whole new vista opened before me, and I knew what to seek and what to shun in the whole long Victorian age.

Another find started an entirely different train of thought. It was an old clay tobacco pipe, its bowl tanned to a deep amber and the tip of its long, thin, curling stem showing signs of having been chewed. Altogether it was rather nasty, and I had no desire to possess it. However, it set me wondering how men lighted pipes before the days of matches and cigarette lighters. I knew that smoking had been something of a ritual in the 18th century when men would sit down for an evening with their pipes, and presumably they put a spill to the flame of a candle, which in turn would be lighted by a spill stuck in the fire. There nearly always was a fire. In some houses the fire in the hall was never allowed to go out, and even on the hottest summer day it would be quietly smouldering, ready to be blown into flame by a pair of bellows. Kitchen fires, too, can seldom have been permitted to go out. But it cannot always have been convenient to go to the hall or the kitchen when you wanted to light a pipe or a candle.

When I began to think about it I realised that every house must have had some means of originating fire, and of course the answer was the tinder box. I had never consciously seen a tinder box so I set out to discover something about them. I happened to be in Wiltshire at the time, so I took the opportunity of going to the fine museum in Salisbury and there I found a most interesting collection of tinder boxes, ranging from the strictly utilitarian kitchen item to the elegant library or drawing room kind.

In essence a tinder box contains four sorts of equipment. There is the flint, the steel, the tinder itself, and some matches. In the simpler kinds, the flint is just a rough stone, split to give a striking surface. The steel is a blade like a miniature chopper with two ears bent over to form a rough handle. The tinder was any old rag, baked perfectly dry ('dry as tinder') in the oven. The matches might be triangles of paper, or slivers of wood but whichever they were the tips would have been dipped in sulphur.

The method was to strike flint and steel against one another, letting the sparks shower on to the tinder. It was a laborious business. There was no instant conflagration, and it took about half a minute of striking away before the tinder began to smoulder. And even then it only smouldered. To get a flame you had to dip the match into it. The essential difference between 18th century matches and those we know today is that the old ones could only be ignited by something which was already burning.

One can find an infinite variety of tinder boxes but they all contain the same ingredients. Sometimes the steel will have a brass handle, or even one of silver or gold. These handles were often elaborate and made in the shape of a dog, presumably because it was easy to hold. The various breeds are accurately represented and so if one is collecting tinder boxes one has the opportunity of dipping into canine history as well.

I have seen one highly ingenious tinder box in which the flint was struck by a mechanical action. The steel was attached to the box with a length of string wrapped round the axle. To work it you pulled the string so that the steel wheel spun and struck the flint on exactly the same principle as a modern cigarette lighter.

The more elegant varieties were tinder pistols which were just like duelling pistols but without barrels. They were common throughout the 18th century and their metal-work was often delicately chased. Clearly the gunsmiths took as much trouble over making tinder pistols as they did over the more lethal kind.

Charred old rags would hardly have been appropriate to such fine workmanship, and a special sort of tinder was developed. Known as 'German tinder' it was, oddly enough, an English export in its raw form. It was compressed fungus, the *polyporus fomentarius,* which grows on old oak, fir, ash, and cherry trees. It was dipped in a solution of nitre and cut into strips and it looked not unlike chamois leather.

Tinder pistols and tinder boxes continued to be made until well into the 19th century. It was not until 1826 that John Walker, a chemist of Stockton-on-Tees, invented the friction match. It was such an enormous improvement on the old method that within a quarter of a century match boxes had almost completely superseded tinder boxes and the only tinder boxes listed in the catalogue of the Great Exhibition of 1851 were described as being 'for explorers' use'.

When I first saw that rather disgusting old 'churchwarden' pipe I little thought that it would send me meandering down the byways of social history to end up at Stockton-on-Tees. But that is the sort of gentle amusement that one can get from poking about museums and antique shops. I did not physically go to Stockton-on-Tees, but another antique oddity really did lead me, over the years, from Dorset to the Lake District. Appropriately enough, it was a device for measuring distances which set me off on this trail.

I was glancing idly through some old documents preserved in a country house in Dorset and I came across an inventory drawn up by the owner when he lent his house to the promising young poet, William Wordsworth, in 1795. Near the end, in the 'Man Servant's Room' was an extraordinary entry – 'A Perambulator in a case'. What on earth, I thought, did a pram case look like? And why have a case at all? Could it be that the flawless copper-plate handwriting had written nonsense? But no, here was Wordsworth himself chipping in with a comment. In a quiet different hand was inscribed 'The handle broken. W.W.' Very wise. Even if you're living rent free you can't be too careful about a possible bill for dilapidations. But the poet evidently had his wits about him and if the inventory said the perambulator had a case, then I could be sure that a case the perambulator had.

145

With a little prompting from the then owner, I realised that it was the reader, not the writer, who was making nonsense. In 1795 a perambulator was not a conveyance for those of gentle years. It was a scientific instrument for recording measurement.

It had other names, too, 'Hodometer', a word which has lost its 'H' and come down to us as 'odometer' to signify the mileage recorder on our car's speedometer. Personally I prefer 'way-wiser', with its overtones of sagacity and its undertones of rebuke to those who tell travellers' tales. But whether called peram-bulator, hodometer or way-wiser, the instrument consisted of a large wheel, about the size of a bicycle wheel, fitted with forks ending in a handle. Below the handle is a dial like a clockface with hour, minute and second hands, each of which records a distance or a total of distances. Looking at the thing head on, the dial is upside down. But when you grasp the handles you look down at the dial from the opposite direction so it is the right way up. The whole thing is made with all the loving care of a fine piece of furniture, and the great instrument-makers of the Age of Reason fashioned them as meticulously and elegantly as their co-craftsman made clocks. And, like the clockmakers, they engraved their names on the brass faces.

There are also much plainer way-wisers. No glass protecting filigree hands, and no filigree hands either. Just stumpy brass digits mounted on the most functional of cases. The reason for this discrepancy is that way-wisers were made for two quite dis-tinct purposes. One was for use by surveyors, and necessarily tough enough to stand up to the mud and muck of road-making.

The other type of way-wiser was equally functional but its task was less exacting. At the end of the 18th and the beginning of the 19th centuries there was a fashion for measuring distances, for fun not for any practical purpose. So, as well as the stern tools of the surveyor, way-wisers were produced to serve as toys for young ladies. So the daintily turned spoke, the fancifully shaped handle, the chased dial, all flourished. There was as much difference between the two as between kitchen and parlour furniture.

I went on rummaging through these old papers to see if I could find other references to the way-wiser and sure enough I did. It wasn't long before Wordsworth's sister, the indomitable Dorothy, stuck her oar in. The owner wrote to his agent and told him to send the perambulator to Sherborne but the agent wrote back saying 'Miss Wordsworth desires it may be delayed till next week that she may measure the distance from this place to Crewkerne'.

The way-wiser on my car made the distance nearly eight miles, and the Dorset-Somerset border is remarkably hilly so the athletic Dorothy Wordsworth cannot have taken less than four or five hours for the round trip. Whether brother William employed this blessed peace in the writing of verse we shall never know. Probably not, because this lovely country sweeping through deep vales to the sea obviously did not move him in the way that the stern grandeur of Westmorland did later.

Whether Dorothy achieved her perambulation is not recorded. But she probably did, she was a forceful young lady, and no less forceful when less young. Anyway, a week later the agent noted in his commopnplace book that he had 'Got the perambulator packed up for the Bakery Man at Clapton to take away in his Cart'. What with all the fuss, the unfortunate agent had obviously had the way-wiser and the Wordsworths in the biggest possible way by this time because he adds 'Whether he will do it or not is a matter of doubt'. Can't you, across the best part of two centuries, hear him sigh with exasperation?

In early Victorian times baby-carriages appeared with enormous wheels and they were derisively heralded as 'perambulators'. The name has stuck, so it's just as well that the original perambulators can fall back on their much nicer name of way-wisers.

A long time after reading those papers I stood beside the tombstone in Grasmere churchyard which marks the graves of William and Dorothy. They had travelled a long way since those early days when the rising young poet had to rely on the bounty of a wealthy patron. But I like to think that their journeyings have been recorded for all time on some celestial way-wiser.

If, like me, you waste a lot of time browsing round antique shops, you will, I hope, be rewarded with many of these mental journeys into the past, and meet some interesting people on the way. For instance, I had no idea that a stool with glass legs would bring me to Benjamin Franklin.

This extraordinary object belonged to an antique dealer.

'It's a lightning stool,' he told me. 'My grandmother used to tell me about them this is the first I've seen. In the 18th century they stood on them during thunderstorms because they thought the glass legs would stop them being struck by lightning.'

It is too facile to say that it wouldn't work. Superstition is a lot stronger than scientific fact, at least it is to the superstitious. In my youth the village women would always buy white heather from the local gypsy because they were afraid that if they didn't she would cast a spell which would make them pregnant. The fact that they became pregnant whether they bought the heather or not did not in the least diminish their firm belief in the gypsy's powers. If that sort of belief can be held in this enlightened age how much more so must it have been two hundred years ago?

I could not very well dimiss the whole thing as an old wives' tale because there stood this lightning stool, or whatever it was, and it undeniably had glass legs. The top was square, under two feet across, and made of mahogany with a rim half an inch high running all round it. The legs, like carrots, were tapering and they were attached to the underside of the top by collars set in battens. The top was highly polished and very slippery so that anybody standing on it would have been in greater danger of breaking a leg than being struck by lightning. Possibly there had originally been a mat, held in place by the rim. Could it really have been a lightning stool? Surely not, but if not what else? It might have been a bed for a small dog but if so why, oh why did it have those glass legs? Of course some very unlikely objects have been made of glass, such as rolling-pins and walking sticks. But legs for a dog's bed? Hardly.

I put the whole mystery out of my mind until one day I saw an engraving of a mid-18th century Frenchman called d'Alibard who was experimenting with lightning conductors. He had a long iron rod mounted on a platform and was holding an earth wire a little distance away. The engraving showed a strong spark leaping between the rod and the earth wire, but what interested me was that the legs of the platform stood in glass bottles.

Now, many amateur scientists in the 18th century had their laboratories beautifully fitted up, and stuffing the legs of a table into bottles would have seemed a very makeshift affair. I felt that I was really on to something at last, and sure enough I discovered that glass-legged stools, known as 'insulating stands' were quite commonly used in 18th century electrical experiments. Whether or not Benjamin Franklin had one I did not manage to discover. But I did discover that, simultaneously with d'Alibard, Franklin was also investigating electricity, and flying kites in thunderstorms to see if he could attract lightning.

But this new – to me – information did not entirely disprove the lightning stool theory. The insulating stands which I subsequently saw were crude unpolished things, and they lacked the rim round the top. They had clearly been made for laboratory use whereas the first stool had equally clearly been made for the parlour.

I doubt if I shall ever know the truth about the lightning stool. But this uncertainty is part of the joy of antique collecting. The more you know about them the more there is to learn. The quest is endless, and so is the enjoyment.

# Index